Artificial Intelligence
from A to Z

Artificial Intelligence from A to Z

Jenny Raggett
and
William Bains

CHAPMAN & HALL
London · New York · Tokyo · Melbourne · Madras

Published by Chapman & Hall, 2–6 Boundary Row, London SE1 8HN

Chapman & Hall, 2–6 Boundary Row, London SE1 8HN, UK

Van Nostrand Reinhold Inc., 115 5th Avenue, New York NY10003, USA

Chapman & Hall Japan, Thomson Publishing Japan, Hirakawacho Nemoto Building, 7F, 1-7-11 Hirakawa-cho, Chiyoda-ku, Tokyo 102, Japan

Chapman & Hall Australia, Thomas Nelson Australia, 102 Dodds Street, South Melbourne, Victoria 3205, Australia

Chapman & Hall India, R. Seshadri, 32 Second Main Road, CIT East, Madras 600 035, India

First edition 1992

© 1992 Jenny Raggett and William Bains

Typeset in 10/12pt Times by Graphicraft Typesetters Ltd., Hong Kong
Printed in Great Britain by Page Bros, Norwich

ISBN 0 412 37950 3   0 442 31200 8 (USA)

A catalogue record for this book is available from the British Library

Library of Congress Cataloging-in-Publication data

Raggett, Jenny.
    Artificial intelligence from A to Z/Jenny Raggett and William Bains.
       p.   cm.
    Includes index.
    ISBN 0–442–31200–8 (pbk.)
    1. Artificial intelligence–Dictionaries. I. Bains, William, 1955– . II. Title.
Q334.2.R34 1992   91–12535
006.3′03–dc20   CIP

Contents

Preface

What is an expert system? How does logic programming work? What is a parser or a natural-language interface? Why the interest in object-oriented programming? What is a neural net? *Artifical Intelligence from A to Z* provides the reader with short non-technical explanations of some 200 terms used in AI and related technologies.

Artificial Intelligence from A to Z is not a textbook for the AI academic: it is not intended for those with an appetite for exhaustive and weighty definitions. The book is written for librarians, lawyers, journalists, consultants, linguists, doctors and a hundred and one other professionals who may encounter AI during the course of their work and want to know what a term means without too much fuss.

As an added bonus, the book does allow you to expand your knowledge on a chosen AI topic. This is done by cross-referencing and reading around the subject. If you originally looked up 'expert system', you will be led to 'knowledge engineering', 'backward chaining', 'explanation system', 'cooperative system' and so on. Similarly, if you look up 'syntax', you may find yourself learning about 'semantics', 'natural-language processing' and 'pragmatics'.

Each entry in the book is marked with a small icon. This tells you in which area of AI the term belongs. From the number of different icons used (there are 12) you will realize that AI permeates into many different fields: it is indeed hard to know where AI starts and where AI ends. AI overlaps with expert-systems technology, computer vision, philosophy, programming techniques, psychology, linguistics and many other disciplines.

Although we have tried to include the terms the reader will most commonly encounter, we have not included by name commercial computer programs based on AI techniques. This is partly to keep the book portable, and partly to avoid having to make contentious (and possibly libellous) comments about commercial software. As a result, any systems we do mention tend to date from the 1970s and early 1980s. These are largely systems designed by academics in the 'golden age' of AI research.

To help you to find the information you want quickly, we have also included an extensive index to the book. This contains not only the names of entries but also any other keywords appearing in the text. Each entry also includes a list of related terms, allowing you to navigate to another topic if you wish.

Foreword

This book offers an accessible introduction to many of the key issues in Artificial Intelligence and associated topics. The short crisp sections give the professional or technical reader quick and clear insight into the meaning of the alphabetically indexed key words. The book's impact is enhanced by the use of drawings and diagrams, and by the many simple examples, some new, some well-known.

The authors have not been shy of the more difficult topics – the highly mathematical subject of neural nets is here freshly and intuitively presented.

If you want more than the usual dictionary definition but do not have time to study research papers, this is the book you need.

Ian Alexander,
Logica

OUR THANKS TO ...

This book is a simplified view of a very technical subject, but it does strive to be right. It would be much less right were it not for the help and encouragement of Martin Lam (consultant), David Raggett and Steven Knight (Hewlett Packard), Mike Gray (IBM), Peter-Fred Thompson (Inmos), Ian Alexander (Logica), David Anderson (PA Consulting Group), Jeremy Bennett, Harry Collins and Geoff Smith (University of Bath). Any errors remaining do so despite, not because of them. We are also grateful to Sheenagh Orchard, to various editors for doing what editors do best (Edit? Ed.), to the incomparable Piers Burnett for 1989, and to our spouses and children for not running off, despite provocation.

ABDUCTION

Logic

Abduction is the sort of reasoning which explains effects in terms of their causes. This contrasts with *deduction*, which works from causes to their inevitable effects. For example, we know that driving a car makes the engine hot. If we open the hood of our Ford and observe the engine to be hot, we can abduce that someone has been driving it. This is not infallible, as there may be other reasons for an engine's being hot. We can gain a numerical estimate of the likelihood of each explanation using *Bayesian logic*, a form of reasoning used in many expert systems.

The most famous user of abduction was the fictitious occupant of 221B Baker Street. Sherlock Holmes almost never used deduction; he reasoned from effects to the (often wildly improbable) events that caused them. That he never made a mistake is indeed, as Dr Watson observed, amazing: real abduction is not that foolproof.

See also: Deduction, Bayes' theorem

1

ALGEBRA

General AI
term

Computer algebra programs were one of the first successful uses of AI techniques. Such programs, or more generally symbolic processing programs, use a range of AI techniques, but particularly logic programming. The father of computer algebra programs is Macsyma, a massive project started in the late 1960s at MIT and still growing. It uses a huge database of mathematical rules, accessed by a relatively simple 'rule manipulator' (similar in concept to the inference engine in a rules-based system), as well as more sophisticated mathematical expertise accessed via expert-system methods.

Computer mathematics programs have scored many successes, including producing a proof of the four-colour theorem (that any map may be coloured with just four colours such that no two adjacent countries have the same colour). Many of their results (and especially the four-colour example) are the result of pedestrian and very time-consuming proofs. Human mathematicians can switch between rule sets, saying things like 'This problem in algebra looks a bit like that one in set theory. I wonder what would happen if ...'. Computer systems have only recently acquired this flexibility.

ALGORITHM

General AI
term

An algorithm is a step-wise method for doing something: for example, 'take a number and double it' or 'put the tea bag in the cup and then add boiling water followed by milk'.

In so-called conventional programming languages like Basic or Cobol, the programmer first devises an algorithm to solve the problem. This is then translated into the programming language, thus enabling the computer to solve the problem too.

Programs developed for AI do not usually put the same emphasis on algorithms. For many of the problems solved by AI techniques, were an algorithm used to solve the problem, it would probably run in what is known as 'exponential time'. This means that, for small problems (for example, timetabling classes for a small school with little choice of subject), the algorithm would function very fast. But for larger problems (timetabling a large school with a choice of 50 subjects) the algorithm would function so slowly as to be wholly impractical.

Human beings do not seem to rely on algorithms for most of the problems they solve; instead, they use less rigorous methods. This is possible because human beings are allowed to make mistakes occasionally. Rules of thumb or heuristics are therefore reasonable substitutes for algorithms even if they occasionally give the wrong result. A doctor uses heuristics to decide that you have flu; you expect him to be right most of the time, but wouldn't be surprised if he were wrong.

AI programs put a similar emphasis on heuristics rather than rigorous step-wise methods.

Although AI techniques do not rely on algorithmic methods in quite the same way as conventional programming, this is not to say that algorithms are not used at all. In search, where the program has to look at a large number of different ways of solving the problem, algorithms are used to make sure that all possible ways of solving the problem are analysed systematically and efficiently until the answer is found.

See also: Combinatorial explosion

3

ALPHA-BETA PRUNING

Search

Alpha-beta pruning is a technique used in computer chess and other gaming programs where the representation involves a search tree with a large number of nodes (see *game tree*). The alpha-beta pruning procedure allows for certain portions of the tree representation to be 'lopped off', on the basis that paths through these portions of the tree are unlikely to lead a player to a win. Pruning makes the search space smaller and easier to deal with.

This idea can be illustrated by looking at the two AND–OR trees below. Given the values of the terminal positions, the values of non-terminal positions are computed by backing up from the terminals by using the minimax procedure. The minimax procedure specifies that, if the tree is drawn from the standpoint of a player 'MAX', then this player, starting at position 1, should move to whichever of positions 2 or 3 has the greatest value to him. Meanwhile player 'MIN', who is assumed to be using the same strategy as player MAX, chooses positions which are of least value to 'MAX' but the greatest value to him.

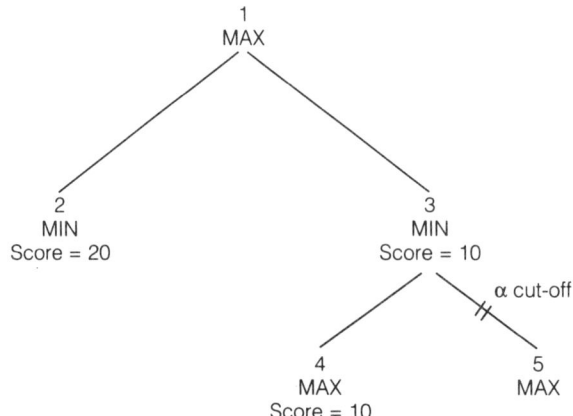

In the example tree above, MAX starts at position 1 and sees that only two positions have been evaluated. He sees that if he moves to position 2, he achieves a position whose score is estimated at 20. If he moves to position 3, however, MIN can then hold him to a score of 10. The value of position 3 is therefore at the most 10, so position 2 is the correct move. The point is that this decision can be made without evaluating position 5 or any of its possible descendants. A portion of the tree can be 'pruned off' as uninteresting at an early stage of search.

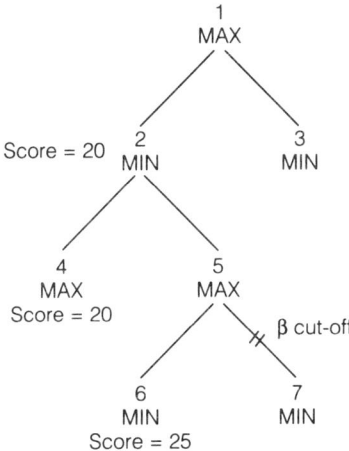

In the second diagram, position 4 has an estimated value of 20. When position 6 is evaluated at 25, it becomes clear that MIN, who always goes for the minimum score, should avoid moving to node 5. This means that position 2 can now be assigned a value of 20; and there is no need to investigate position 7 or any of its descendants. Again, a portion of the tree can be 'pruned off'.

The alpha-beta technique uses two parameters, alpha and beta. In the first case the parameter alpha takes the lower limit of 20 on MAX's achievement as he moves from position 1. In the second case the parameter beta is set to 20, representing the upper limit on the value to MAX of position 2. The elimination of node 7 is a beta cut-off.

See also: Chess, Search

ALVEY

Funding

Alvey has in common with Wellington, Brougham and Mae West the fact that their names have all come to represent the creation with which they were associated. The Alvey committee (named after its Chairman, John Alvey) recommended in 1983 a collaborative programme of research and development in Britain to respond to the Japanese Fifth Generation Projects initiative. Funded by the British government, ALVEY grew to a £350 million programme covering software engineering, very large-scale integration (VLSI), intelligent knowledge-based systems (IKBS) and the man-machine interface (MMI).

ALVEY provided an enormous boost to the UK research community, and elements of it succeeded in spreading awareness of new techniques. However, British industry was not as enthusiastic as its Japanese counterparts and the Government decided against a follow-up, relying instead on the normal research budgets of the Department of Trade and Industry and the Science and Engineering Research Council, together with the support likely to be forthcoming to British participants in ESPRIT.

See also: Fifth-generation projects, ESPRIT

AND- OR TREE

Search

An AND–OR tree is one of many representations of the stages or intermediate states in solving a problem. It consists of a tree in which every node, or point of branching, represents a sub-problem of the whole. For example, consider the problem of getting a robot to pick up a cup of some hot drink in the kitchen and carry it to the dining-room table. The problem can be reduced to a number of sub-problems so that the search tree can be represented as follows:

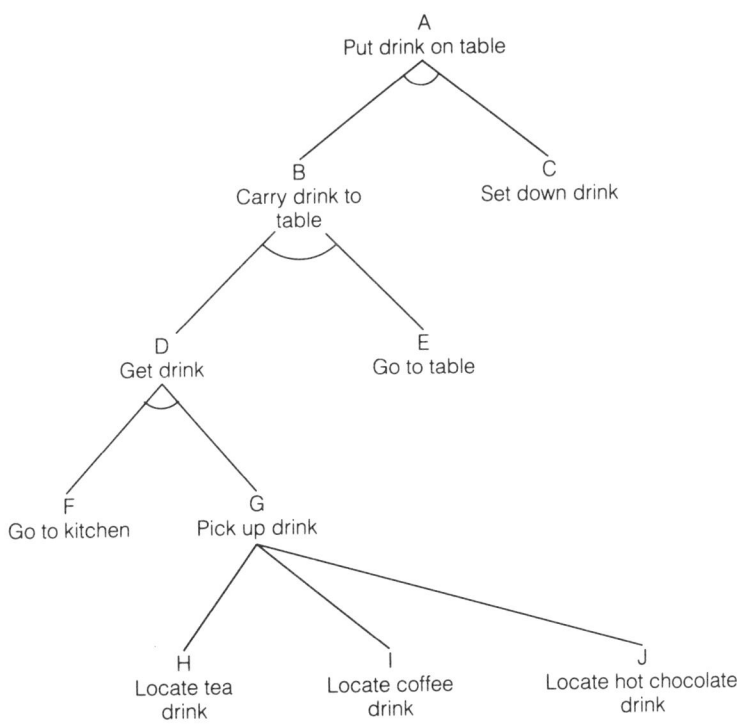

In this representation, node A is an AND expansion: you need to do B AND C before A is accomplished. Node G is an OR expansion: accomplishing either sub-problem H OR I OR J is sufficient. The convention for representing AND and OR nodes is shown below.

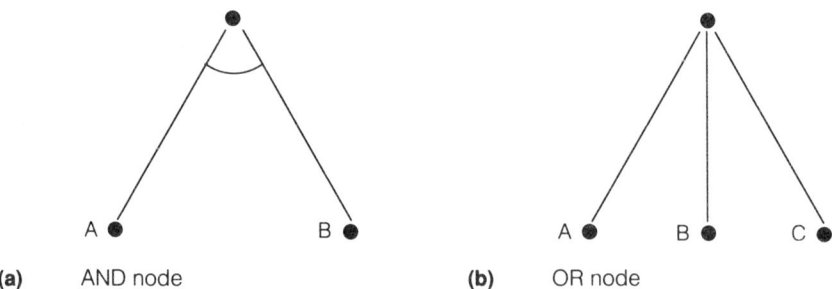

(a)   AND node   **(b)**   OR node

AND–OR trees can be searched breadth first, depth first or with the aid of heuristics in the usual way.

The search for the winning move in a game may be represented by an AND–OR tree. The nodes in the tree correspond to the board positions, with the root being the start position and the leaves of the tree corresponding to positions in which the game is over. The AND expansions represent the opponent's move; the OR expansions the player's move. See *game tree* for a more detailed explanation of this idea.

See also: Alpha-beta pruning, Search

ANNEALING

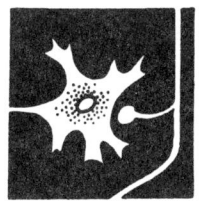

Neural nets

Simulated annealing is a method for solving problems using highly parallel computers. It is still a research tool, although it shows promise for the future.

Annealing is a variation on 'hill-climbing' problem-solving methods, and gets around the problem of 'local optimal solutions'. The approach is modelled on what happens during the metallurgical process of annealing. Metals are heated to a little below their melting point and then cooled slowly: this gives all their atoms time to settle down into place, leaving none misplaced. The computational analogy is a variant on hill-climbing methods for solving problems, which introduces random 'noise' – the computational equivalent of heat – into the calculation. This is a potential method for preventing the program being stuck in local optima: the noise can jiggle them out again. However, the method is very time-consuming, and hence only practical on massively parallel computers. Annealing methods have been applied to optimizing the performance of neural networks.

A computer dedicated to problem-solving using simulated annealing is called a *Boltzmann machine*, after the physicist Ludwig Boltzmann.

See also: Hill climbing, Neural nets

ARGUMENT

General
computer
term

The word 'argument' is used in AI as follows.

1. In predicate calculus, an argument refers to one of the items about which a proposition makes an assertion. For example, in the proposition

   IN (CAT, ROOM)

   CAT and ROOM are the arguments of the predicate IN.

2. The word 'argument' may also be used in a similar way to 'parameter'. For example, in Lisp, the arguments of a procedure are the items it will take and process. Thus a Lisp procedure PRINT might take as its arguments the words of a sentence and print them out on paper.
3. A third use of 'argument' is in mathematical logic. Given that certain facts, or 'propositions' are jointly true, other propositions may be deduced in consequence. The rules that enable you to deduce new propositions from those known already, are known as 'argument forms'. A classic argument form is *modus ponens* (see *Deduction*).

ASSERTION

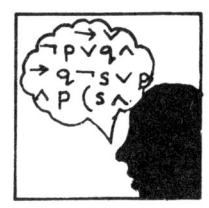

Logic

An assertion is a simple statement of fact, which, as far as the program is concerned, is true. For example:

I like fish.
I like milk.
Cats like milk and fish.

In logic programming, a program consists of a number of assertions of a simple type, describing relationships between objects and ideas. When the program is 'run', new facts may be derived and, in turn, asserted also. Thus the program, using the facts above, might assert:

I am a cat.

See also: Logic programming, Declarative programming language

ATOM

General
computer
term

Originally entering AI as a Lisp term, 'atom' is used elsewhere (in Prolog, for example) to mean the smallest, indivisible statement or unit of a programming language. In Lisp an atom is the simplest thing you can have: the name for something (i.e. the symbol associated with it). Thus '1' is the symbol associated with the number 1, and is an atom.

Atoms are what are combined to make a list. Not everything in a list is an atom, though: it can comprise other lists. Thus the list

(Macdonald's farm (pigs cows sheep hens))

contains three elements but only two atoms ('Macdonald's' and 'farm'); the other element is itself a list. This list (pigs cows sheep hens) itself contains four atoms.

See also: Lisp

AUGMENTED
TRANSITION
NETWORK

NLP

Some of the best-known natural-language front ends are based on a method of processing sentences called an augmented transition network, or ATN.

When you hear the word 'the', you naturally expect the next word to be a noun or an adjective. If the second word is an adjective, you then expect another adjective or a noun to follow. Thus you anticipate the structure of the sentence and slot in words accordingly.

ATNs are based on this idea. The structure of sentences in computerized form is represented as a network of nouns, adjectives, verbs and so on. In addition, there are routes marked through the network, and these correspond to legitimate sequences of words the network will accept.

In the network below, the parser (a program which analyses a sentence), begins at the position 'start'. It then proceeds along the arc labelled 'article' (corresponding to an 'a' or a 'the') as it recognizes the first word. At the central box, one or more adjectives are acceptable. To get to the last box and thence to the finish, a noun and then a verb are required.

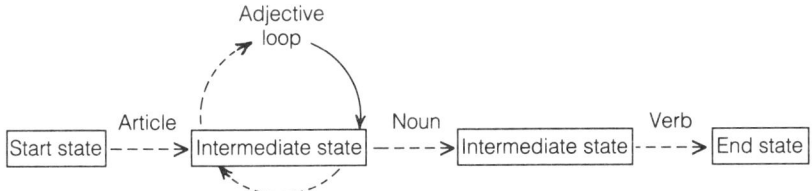

Acceptable sentences to the network above might include the following

The woolly white sheep jumps.
A big white woolly cat eats.

Networks used in real natural-language applications are, of course, a lot more complicated than this. Several networks may be linked together, and the sentence may be 'handed' from one network to another as different parts (noun phrase, verb phrase and so on) are parsed. Role registers keep track of current candidates of 'parts of speech' where these are not immediately obvious. This enables the subject, say, of a sentence to be found even when the structure of the sentence is complicated. Feature registers keep track of properties of individual words: for example, whether nouns are singular or plural. An augmented transition network goes further than classifying words as one or other type: it expects nouns and verbs to agree and uses the endings of words to gain insight into the meaning of sentences.

The main limitation of ATNs is their inflexibility. An ATN parser only accepts a sentence once it has arrived at an end state. If the parser fails to arrive at an end state by one route or another, it has to backtrack and try another route. The number of routes grows exponentially with the size of the network, so for complex sentences as many as 600 routes may need to be tried before the sentence is parsed. Of course, in some cases, the sentence will fall outside the ATN grammar and not be parsed at all.

See also: Parser, Natural-language processing, Grammar

AUTOMATIC PROGRAMMING

General AI
term

In automatic programming (AP), the computer is used to help write programs. It can allow the user to specify a program in a higher-level language, or it can allow some ambiguity in that specification. Once a program is exactly specified, translating (or compiling) the specification into a known computer language is relatively straightforward. Methods for specification can be as follows.

1. *Formal.* This is analogous to (but stricter than) traditional programming; the specification is stated in a formal language such as predicate calculus. This allows the logical structure of a program to be stated succinctly without bothering with mechanical details of how the program is going to work.
2. *By example.* We give some example of what the program is to do, and the computer then writes the program to do it. However, the specification is rarely complete. There are many paths from any input to any output, but only one will give the right result with a completely different input. This is a problem with all forms of induction.
3. *Through natural language.* This is the most attractive option for 'non-programmers' writing programs. It is often interactive as the program seeks to remove ambiguities and gaps in the initial specification by asking questions about key areas.
4. *By graphical description.* Using little pictures ('icons') on the screen to describe the program elements and using a WIMPS interface to select icons, draw lines between them and so on.

AP is still a research subject in many respects, although some output has seen general use in compiler-interpreter combinations in AI environments. There are a wide number of approaches using logic programming, knowledge engineering or problem-solving methods. The problems they address are partial information in a specification, inconsistency in a specification, and efficiency of the final program. A relatively new approach to automatic programming is to avoid any rigorous definition and use a genetic algorithm to evolve it statistically.

See also: Learning

AUTOMATON

Theory/
Philosophy

In computer science, an automaton is a very simple computer. It has a very small memory, usually one that can record only a few bits of information, an input (often a 'tape' of symbols), and a set of rules about what it can do in response to particular input symbols, depending on its internal state. Such automata are called 'finite-state automata' because of their finite, indeed very limited, number of internal states, as compared with the potentially infinite program that they read off the 'tape'.

Automata are used as 'thought experiment' computers to try to imagine what things computers can and cannot do. Turing showed that some sorts of simple automaton are equivalent to any discrete computer, if they have a complicated enough program. Thus they are mathematical models for bigger, more realistic computers. Any automaton which can do this, i.e. which can act as a mathematical model of a real digital machine, is said to have full computational power. Any problem which can be solved by a computer with full computational power can be solved by any suitable computer: conversely, if it cannot be solved by one, it cannot be solved by a digital computer at all.

See also: Turing machine

BACK PROPAGATION

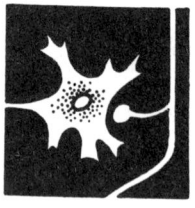

Neural nets

This is a method of learning used in neural nets with more than two layers of neurons, i.e. with 'hidden layers'. For a given input pattern, the actual output is compared with the desired output. The difference between the two is then 'propagated' back into whatever connections were used to get that output in the first place. If the match is good, then the units which contributed to the output get their connections strengthened. If the match is bad, then

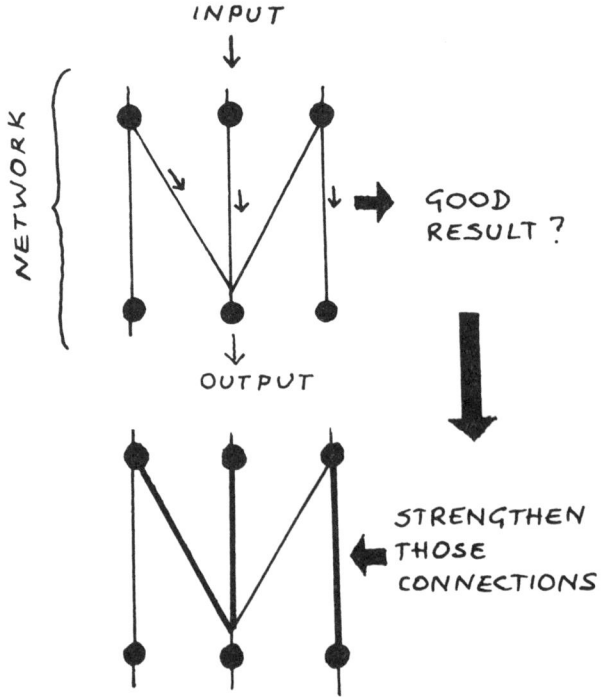

the connections between the units concerned are reduced in strength; next time those particular input units fire up, they will have less effect on the hidden and output units than before. In a recent variation, the hidden layer automatically feeds back to the input layer to perform this adjustment, a method called a 'recirculation algorithm'.

This method of learning by reinforcement shows some of the characteristics of human learning, particularly of how young children overgeneralize rules of grammar when they learn to speak. 'I goed to the shops with mummy' a $2\frac{1}{2}$-year-old might say, not realizing that 'go' has its own, irregular past tense.

Back propagation is restricted to cases where the net is already near to its 'goal', or on a continuous path to it. For the cases where these conditions do not apply, annealing methods may have to be used.

See also: Connectionism, Neural nets

BACKTRACKING

Search

Backtracking is a term associated with search. In many programs where the computer has to explore a search space and, in the process, make choices, backtracking allows it to 'try again' once it has made a mistake.

In logic programming, backtracking is especially important when searching out every possible solution to a conjunctive condition. For example, take the following rule.

Y is the daughter of X if:

X is the mother of Y

condition 1

and Y is female.

condition 2

The database tells us that:

Katherine is the mother of Edward;
Katherine is the mother of Rose;
Henry is the father of John;
Ann is the mother of John;
Henry is the father of Edward;
Rose is the mother of Sally.

Mary is female;
Katherine is female;
Ann is female;
Rose is female;
Henry is male;

John is male;
Edward is male;
Sally is female.

As the computer searches for mother-daughter relationships, it 'binds' the variables X and Y to symbols from the database. Each part of the conjunctive condition is dealt with in turn; therefore you might imagine the computer binding X to Katherine and Y to Edward as a first attempt.

Upon evaluating the second condition, however, this combination obviously fails as Edward is a male, and not a female as required. The program therefore backtracks and undoes the binding to Edward.

On the next attempt, the computer binds X to Katherine and Y to Rose. The conjuctive condition is satisfied. All other combinations of variables to bind to X and Y are discovered before proceedings are stopped.

Backtracking is also used more generally in search. A search tree may be investigated using depth-first or breadth-first search. In the former case, the search tree is searched from the root to the tips of the branches, either left to right or right to left. If the search reaches the tip of a branch without successfully finding the solution to the problem, then the program 'backtracks' and a fresh branch is tried.

See also: Depth-first search, Prolog

BACKWARD CHAINING

Expert
systems

Backward chaining is a method used by many AI systems to solve problems. The principle is similar to that used in the game of 'Twenty Questions'. The computer starts by setting a particular conclusion. It then attempts to establish whether or not that conclusion is justified by asking questions, as follows.

Hypothesis: I think the disease you've got is chicken-pox.

So ask: Are the spots red with a small white blister in the middle?
Are you a small child or baby?
Is this the first time in your life that you have had these symptoms?

In AI, the hypothesis is sometimes known as the 'goal'. The facts needed for the hypothesis to be true are known as its 'conditions'. Backward chaining is said to be goal-orientated: the computer specifies a goal first and then uses facts and rules to determine whether or not the goal can be achieved.

The opposite of backward chaining is forward chaining. This is said to be 'data-driven': the system first looks at the information it possesses and then looks at what conclusions can be made.

Typically, a program using backward chaining consists of a series of conditional rules, as follows.

A if B and C   mammal if rodent or cow
B if D and E   rodent if small furry animal and squeaks
C if X and Y   cow if vegetarian and says moo
X if R and S   vegetarian if never eats meat and never eats fish

A backward-chaining algorithm would provide a way of methodically applying each rule in turn.

Conditional rules are sometimes described in terms of the consequent (what happens when the rule fires as the conditions are met) and an antecedent (the conditions themselves). Using this terminology, backward chaining involves successively taking the antecedents of one rule and making these, in turn, the consequents of other rules. The process stops when the antecedents of one rule cannot be further redefined.

See also: Forward chaining, Search, Expert systems

BAYESIAN LOGIC

Logic

Bayes' theorem is a way of working out the most likely reason for something. It allows us to relate effects to their causes using the probability that particular causes have particular effects. This is *a posteriori* logic: we want to work out the cause of something after we have seen its effect.

This sort of reasoning could be very useful for expert systems, as we often know what the chances are that a given cause will have a given effect *in general* without knowing the likelihood of that cause being the explanation in a *particular* case. (In practice this is quite hard to do.) Bayes' theorem also allows you to calculate the likelihood if there are many factors involved: combinations of this sort are the basis of reasoning in Bayesian logic. In an expert system using Bayesian logic the list of probabilities will constitute a database on which the expert system will act, generating numerical as well as logical answers. The medical diagnosis systems ONCOCIN, QMR, INTERNIST and MYCIN use variations on this sort of logic, as do many simpler systems for diagnosing the causes of problems from their observed effects. The probabilities in Bayesian logic also crop up as certainty factors in some knowledge-engineering contexts.

See also: Certainty, Deduction, Expert systems

BELIEF

Theory/
Philosophy

Much of AI is about knowledge. However, much of human discourse and most of the most enduring human achievements concern beliefs. AI research has attempted to model belief as well as knowledge, for three reasons. Belief has a key role in some forms of knowledge acquisition, especially *induction*, where a belief about the subject is formed before full knowledge is, or can be, acquired. Related to this is the importance of computer understanding of belief to human-computer communications, particularly in computer-aided learning. Related to this in turn is the more general attempt to understand human belief.

Belief systems (both collections of beliefs, like Buddhism, and computer systems which models some aspect of belief) have a number of peculiarities which distinguish them from knowledge systems.

1. Two belief systems can come to quite different conclusions based on the same facts. (See *paradigm* for the importance of this to understanding and knowledge.) They are 'non-consensual' (i.e. do not come to a consensus).
2. They frequently deal with abstracts that may not be shared between systems. For example, there is a deep division in philosophy about whether the phrase 'machine intelligence' actually means anything. If you do not believe that there can be any such thing as 'machine intelligence', then discussing whether a computer has it is futile. Often these abstract entities include some equivalent of 'good' and 'bad'. This contrasts with knowledge systems, which, if they are about the same subject, must discuss the same thing.
3. Belief systems are often about non-existent worlds ('In an ideal world...').
4. Belief is not connected to facts in a straightforward way.
5. Credibility and emotion are as relevant to the 'proof' of a belief as logic.
6. Belief is to do with desire (conation) rather than reasoning (cognition).

The last point puts belief at odds with nearly all other AI development. Belief is about what we *want* to be true, not what is true. This was demonstrated by PARRY, a program that simulated a paranoid. The program brought any discussion round to the point of its obsessions (the Mafia), regardless of the subject, and avoided certain other 'sensitive' topics. The program would even 'lie' to preserve its belief structure. The implications of this were widely misunderstood (and were not helped by a crude quasi-natural-language front end), as most AI researchers thought that PARRY was an attempt to model cognition (as are most AI systems) rather than conation.

See also: Explicit v. tacit knowledge

BINARY IMAGE

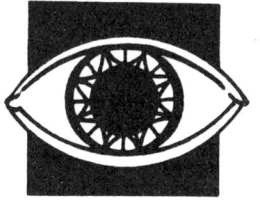

Vision

A binary image is one that consists of only two colours, usually black and white. This means that it can be represented directly by binary numbers: for example, 1 for white and 0 for black (or vice versa).

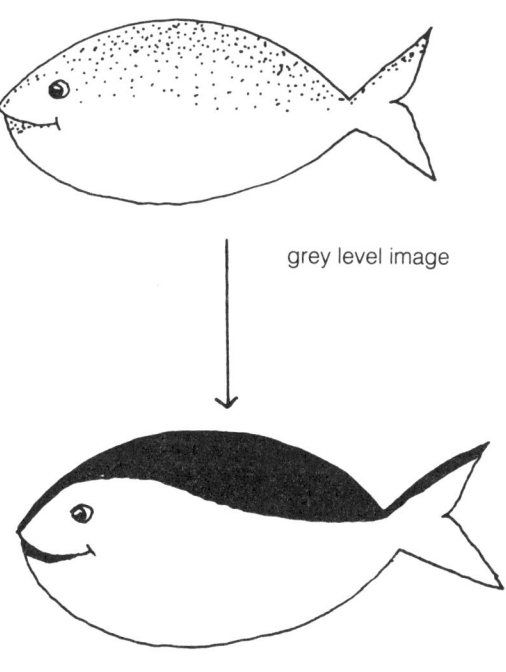

grey level image

binary image

BLOCKS WORLD

Games and
toy domains

Blocks world is one of the simplified versions of the world on which AI programs or methods are tested: it is a 'toy domain'. The original blocks world consists of square blocks that sit on a flat table; the blocks can be stacked up on top of each other or on the table. Thus it can be characterized very simply by describing which blocks are on top of which other blocks. This is a simple 'test-bed' for algorithms which reason about logical statements. This was seen as the start of a system of reasoning about how the world was put together, which could be expanded for use by robots and computer-vision systems.

They were later generalized to three-dimensional versions containing regular geometrical shapes. A famous use was in Terry Winograd's paper 'Understanding natural language', in which the user conversed with the SHRDLU program about a blocks world of coloured boxes, blocks and pyramids. This simulated world was manipulated by a simulated robot arm following user instructions in English. The robot arm would pick up, move and put down blocks, and under the direction of SHRDLU disassemble piles of blocks or make towers, explaining as it went why it was performing specific moves. Hailed as a major breakthrough at the time, its lack of generality has since proved a major drawback, as has also proved true of other blocks-world programs.

BOOLEAN ALGEBRA

Theory/
Philosophy

In his book, *An Investigation into the Laws of Thought on which Are Founded the Mathematical Theories of Logic and Probabilities*, George Boole (in 1854) set out the rules for logical operations, based on the connectives AND, OR and NOT. He showed how the inherent truth or falsity of statements could be demonstrated by manipulating symbols standing for those propositions. This, then, is symbolic logic: just as

$a + b = c$

is a symbolic sum, with a, b and c symbolizing numbers, so

a AND b NOT c

is a symbolic argument, where b, for example, symbolizes a logical statement such as 'The cow is brown' or 'All men are mortal'.

	True	False
True	True	False
False	False	True

← statement 1

↑ statement 2

A basic tool of Boolean algebra is the *truth table*. Just as a multiplication table gives the numerical result of multiplying two numbers, so a truth table gives the 'truth' value of performing logical operations on statements. Conventionally 'true' is represented by '1' and 'false' by '0' in such tables.

Boolean algebra has been used extensively in computer logic, especially in its application in *propositional calculus*.

See also: Deduction, Propositional calculus

BREADTH FIRST SEARCH

Search

Many problems can be represented, for the purpose of computerization, as a search tree. A search tree shows, for a particular problem, the stages in solving it as a number of 'nodes'. Lines between nodes symbolize 'operators'. These are procedures or actions which have been applied to move from one stage in solving the problem to another stage.

Breadth-first and depth-first search are two techniques for searching methodically through nodes in a search tree. To illustrate what is involved in breath-first search, consider a computer wanting to get from San Francisco to Nice in France by plane.

The information the computer knows about the routes between the various places is represented as a tree to be searched. The search begins at San Francisco. As a first step, the computer generates all successors to this, the 'root' node. Successor nodes constitute level 1 nodes. These consist of London and Frankfurt, towns one stop away from the root. Since neither of the towns at level 1 matches the goal (Nice), the computer generates level 2 nodes, towns which are two stops away from San Francisco.

This process of generating new nodes, level by level, continues until Nice is found. The computer can then pin-point the shortest and most direct route to its Mediterranean destination.

In a search tree with lots of branches, breadth-first search can take a very long time. More importantly, breadth-first search can take up a lot of computer memory. This is because, as the search proceeds, all the nodes at a particular level have to be stored at once. In our example, all nodes at level 3 would have to be saved in their entirety while level 4 nodes were being generated.

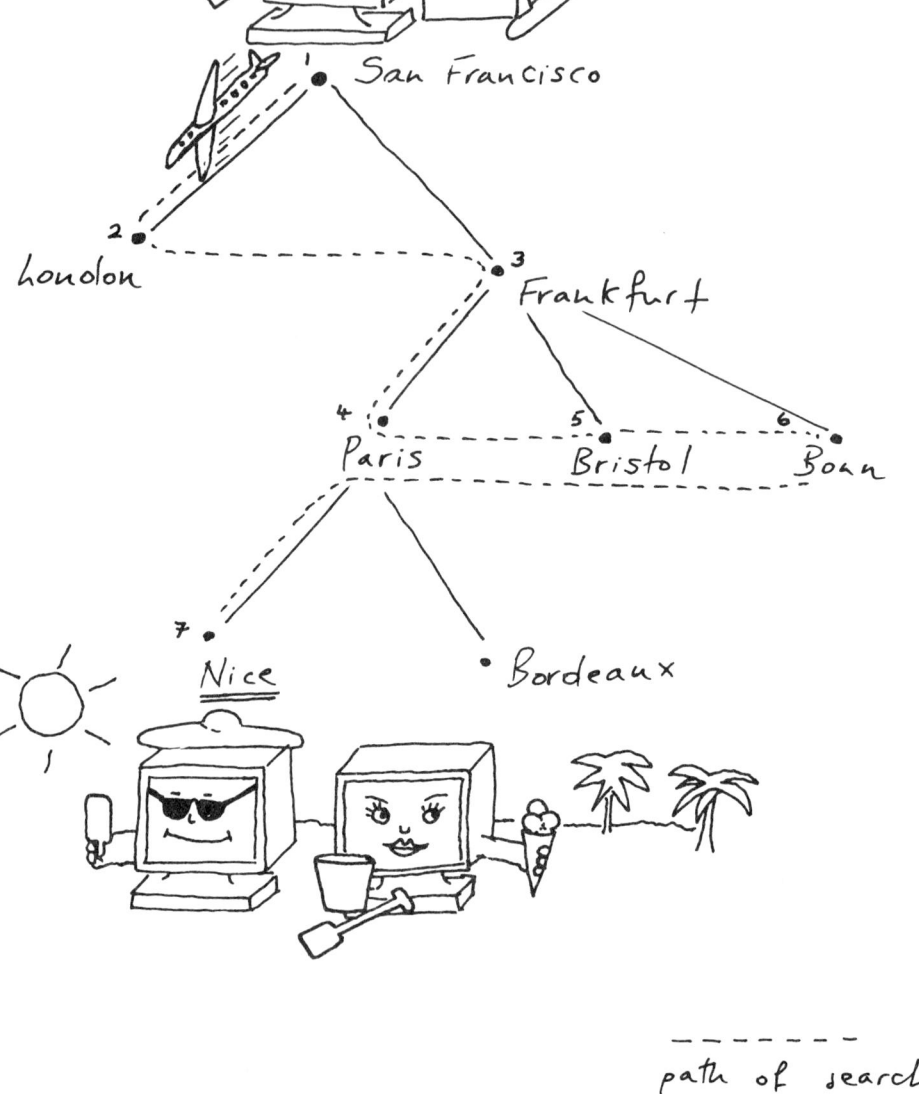

San Francisco

London

Frankfurt

Paris

Bristol

Bonn

Nice

Bordeaux

path of search

As a result of its heavy use of memory, breadth-first search may, in practice, use up available memory in seconds.

See also: Search, Depth-first search

CASE GRAMMAR

NLP

A case grammar is a method of representing the concepts underlying a sentence. The word 'case' is used here differently from its traditional use in, for example, Latin where it refers to the surface appearance of words, whether they are in the nominative, genitive or so on. A case in the context of natural-language processing gives more specific information on the role that a word plays in a sentence. Common cases therefore include such concepts as:

Agent:	the thing that caused an action to occur;
Object:	the thing that is acted upon;
Instrument:	a tool used by the agent;
Source and destination:	places where an object is moved from and to.

To give the computer a clue as to what a sentence actually means, words in the sentence can be slotted into a frame-like representation based on the idea of a case.

Consider the following sentence:

Eleanor made the house using Lego bricks.

Its corresponding frame might be:

Verb:	made;
Object:	the house;
Agent:	Eleanor;
Instrument:	Lego bricks.

See also: Grammar, Natural-language processing

33

CELLULAR AUTOMATON

Theory/
Philosophy

This is a type of automaton which uses an array of cells as both memory and processing elements. The best known is John Conway's game of Life, which is played on an infinite square board. Each square (cell) can contain a counter, or be empty. On each go (generation) the player fills or empties squares depending on three simple rules. If played by a computer at several generations per second, this makes a fascinating display, which accounts for some of this automaton's popularity.

Many cellular automata have full computational power, and so can be used to investigate aspects of computer theory. In addition, they are similar to neural nets in being made up of a large number of very simple units whose activity is determined by that of other units, and so they can be theoretical models for non-von Neumann computers as well as conventional ones.

See also: Automaton

CERTAINTY

General AI
term

Certainty factors are measures of how sure we are that a fact is right, and are used in automatic reasoning systems, such as expert systems, which have to deal with uncertain information. In some expert systems certainty factors represent the degree of belief that we want to attach to some assertion. They are usually on a scale of 1 (complete certainty that a fact is true) to 0 (complete uncertainty), or to −1 (complete certainty that the fact is false).

Certainty factors can be related to the probability that a fact is true. If they are so used, they can be used in statistical calculations (similar to Bayesian logic calculations) to combine incompatible assertions like the following to provide consistent, although only statistically reliable, answers.

Assertion	Certainty
My aunt lives in the city	0.7
Bulls live in the country	0.9
My aunt has just seen a bull	0.5

(We are fairly confident that all bulls live in the country, but not so sure that my aunt lives in the city, and not at all convinced that my aunt knows a bull from a bullfrog.)

See also: Bayesian logic, Expert systems

CHAOS

Theory/
Philosophy

Chaos is a fashionable mathematical term that has found its way into AI. It is a way of describing apparently unpredictable systems. Chaos theory may have applications in neural net and genetic algorithm approaches, and more generally may describe basic features of intelligence.

In a *determined system*, such as a swinging pendulum, the state the system is in exactly determines what state it is going to be in next. In a simple system, if we are told what state the system is in now, we can simply calculate what state the system will be in in a moment's time, and at any time in the future. In a *chaotic system*, the state it will be in in a moment is still predictable, but where it will be in the more distant future is almost impossible to predict. This is because tiny differences in the system's current state can make a very big difference to its future state. The executive toy that has a pendulum swinging over magnets is like this. Whereas a regular pendulum will swing in a predictable way, a pendulum that is being pulled about by magnets will swing in an erratic and random way, never repeating the same path. If you started out from *exactly* the same position, the pendulum would trace out the same path. But even a hair's breadth difference in the starting position will result in drastically different paths.

Both determined and chaotic systems are to be distinguished from a *random system*, in which the current state is not the only influence on future ones.

CHESS

Games and
toy domains

The earliest record of a chess-playing automaton was around 1800 when a man called Van Kempelen exhibited an automaton dressed as a Turk, seated at a chess board. The Turk won chess games all over Europe and many were very impressed. It was eventually discovered that the automaton was a human dwarf in disguise.

Research into chess-playing programs took off properly in the 1950s when Lex Bernstein achieved the goal of a program which rated just above 500 in one of the ranking systems used in chess (see below).

A beginner playing legal chess	500
Quite good player	1200
Internationally ranked player	2000
Grand master	3000+

In 1967, a program written by Richard Greenblatt achieved a ranking of about 1100. Later, in 1972, a program called Chess 3.6, invented by David Slate and Larry Atkin at Northwestern University in the USA, rated at 1400. A later version of the program, Chess 4.0, scored 2070 on a faster computer. The 1982 computer chess champion, Belle, ranked about 2300. Deep Thought, a whole computer system (its hardware and software are designed with chess in mind) ranks about 2550. Deep Thought is the work of F.H. Hsu and Thomas Anantharaman at Carnegie Mellon University.

How do chess game programs work? Given the number of possible courses of play that may follow from any particular point in the game, exhaustive generation and search of all the repercussions of all the possible moves the computer could make is impossible.

This means that some method of limiting the amount of search the computer has to do is an essential part of getting the computer to play chess. The challenge of finding the right move, given the extremely large search space involved, still faces AI researchers in chess.

37

The first consideration is how many nodes in the game tree you want to search. Two things must be controlled: width and depth. Programs which perform full-width search explore very large search trees of hundreds of thousands of nodes. This is only practical on a large and very expensive computer. Smaller computers use *fan-out parameters*, which limit the width of the tree to be investigated at certain depths.

The *alpha-beta pruning* procedure is another technique used to limit the number of nodes searched. Essentially, this tells the computer to prune branches of the search tree according to calculations that show those branches do not contain any good moves.

Meanwhile, *quiescent search* involves considering only those positions that are certain to be correctly estimated in their outcome. Moves which give an unpredictable result (moves which may give the computer a sudden advantage in the game, but may have the reverse effect in unlucky circumstances) are not considered in the search.

A second consideration in search is the choice of the most promising node to expand. This is done by the use of *heuristics*: rules of thumb that are used to estimate whether a move is a good or a bad one. Heuristics allow one, for example, to judge a position by whether pieces would be lost or gained, whether pieces would be threatened by pins or forks, whether the move brings a queen, rook or bishop into the game, and so on. Computers using heuristics can make the search space smaller as certain moves are discredited.

Other techniques to limit search involve using knowledge of past chess games. A game of chess only involves, say, a hundred moves. To store an entire sequence of moves in a database is relatively easy: all you have to do is to store the coordinates of the pieces on the board. A hash table (a table which uses a single number to sum up all the positions on the board) is then used to index each of these snapshots of the game, allowing the computer very quickly to scan and test if the position it is currently dealing with matches a position previously encountered.

This means that the computer could recognize any board position that has been played by any of the grand masters in the past century. It could find out, given a difficult position to deal with, how a grand master might respond. Or, given that a grand master had failed by responding with a particular move, the computer could rule that move out.

At least half the progress in computer chess since 1974 is attributable to the sheer power of computer hardware. Computers can now search faster and deeper than ever before. In the computer chess system Deep Thought, specialized chips are customized to be good at different aspects of search. Seven VLSI chips handle look-up tables in which basic features of chess games are represented. These include, for example, the patterns of pawns on the board, and their significance. Although Deep Thought can easily outdo grand masters when it comes to depth and accuracy of tactical look-ahead, it can still be beaten by superior strategic long-term plots on the part of the human player.

See also: Search, Alpha-beta pruning, Minimax technique

CHINESE ROOM

Theory/
Philosophy

The Chinese room is an analogy of AI, and more specifically of natural-language processing. It was invented by John Searle to show that AI is not true intelligence, but a simulation of it.

Imagine a man standing in a room containing a large book. The man understands no Chinese, but the book contains a large set of rules about Chinese characters. The rules might say that, if you see a particular combination of characters followed by a given combination, then write this character and push it through the letterbox in the door.

We, the experimenters (who can understand Chinese), stand outside the room. First we put a story written in Chinese into the room. Then we put in a series of questions also in Chinese. The man looks at the characters input as a story and the characters input as questions, looks up characters in his book, and outputs them. And out come the answers in Chinese. But, argues Searle, all the man inside does is to carry out instructions that in a given circumstance he should do a specific thing. The symbols have no meaning for him. There is no understanding, just the simulation of understanding.

The analogy with expert systems and natural-language processing is clear. These systems, especially rule-based systems, are equivalent to the big book of rules, which the computer operates without any 'understanding', and have only a simulation of intelligence.

Of course, the same argument may be applied to people: my observation that you produce a relevant reply when I ask you a question is no reason for supposing that you have understood a word I am saying.

A reply to this argument, described in more detail in *The Mind's I* by Douglas Hofstadter and Daniel Dennett, is the *system argument*, which says that the intelligence lies not in the individual components of the room any more than it does in individual neurons in our brains, but in the configuration of the system as a whole.

See also: Simulation v. emulation

CLASSIC PUZZLES

Games
and toy
domains

Several puzzles have become 'classic' tests for aspects of AI. They are distinguished from toy domains because puzzles are not meant to represent the real world.

1. *Cannibals and missionaries*. Two cannibals and two missionaries have to cross a river, using a boat that only holds two people. Only missionaries can row, and if cannibals outnumber missionaries on either bank then they eat the missionaries. What sequence of transfers is required? This is a simple problem which can be explored by breadth- or depth-first exploration of a state graph.
2. *Chess* (also chequers or draughts). In both cases, there is more than one type of 'piece' moving on an 8 × 8 board in a game between two players.
3. *Eight-square*. A 3 × 3 square contains eight 1 × 1 square pieces labelled 1–8 or A–H, and one gap. Initially the pieces are randomly arranged. By moving selected pieces into the gap, the player has to arrange them into ascending or descending order. The object is to do this in as few moves as possible. A related game is Rubik's cube, which is a three-dimensional version in which sub-cubes with different coloured faces have to be assembled into a cube with each face all of the same colour by rotation of groups of sub-cubes.
4. *Go*. A tactical game between two players. Each player takes turns in placing a 'stone' of their colour on a chequered board. When an area is enclosed by a player, all the stones in that area are 'captured' by that player, and so become that player's colour. The object is to end up with most stones of 'your' colour. Go has very few rules, but because of the vast number of possible moves at each step the state space for Go is vast.
5. *Nim*. There are two players, and a stack of pennies (or a collection of stones/counters), traditionally at least five. The players take turns at removing one, two or three pennies from the stack. The player who removes the last penny loses. This game is a good test case for finding

a winning strategy, i.e. one which forces your opponent to lose. Because it is simple, the entire search tree (= state tree = game tree) can be constructed and searched.

6. *Noughts and crosses* (also called tic-tac-toe). Two players take turns to mark a circle (for one player) or a cross (for the other) on the blank spaces of a 3 × 3 board. The first to make a line of three circles or crosses wins. This is another game for testing procedures for exhaustive searches of search trees or for 'pruning', and for searching for a winning strategy.

7. *Tower of Hanoi*. The board has three pegs on it, and on the left-hand peg there are a number of discs stacked in size order, smallest uppermost. In the original version, claimed to be an aid to Buddhist meditation, there are 64 discs. The object is to transfer all the discs to the right-most peg by moving only one disc at a time and never putting a disc on top of a smaller disc. Like the *travelling salesman problem*, the state graph of this problem expands enormously as the number of discs increases. Because it is characterized by only two simple rules, it is well suited to production rule type and Prolog-based games programs. Fisher-Price markets a version for toddlers.

See also: Chess, Search

CLOSED-WORLD ASSUMPTION

Search

The closed-world assumption assumes the knowledge represented in a system to be absolutely complete. Like the final stages of a detective novel, since every possible fact has been stated, it is simply a matter of logic to examine the evidence and come up with the inevitable conclusion.

In mathematical logic, you assume that the axioms of an argument present all the facts needed to arrive at a conclusion: the world of mathematical logic is 'closed'. Real life is certainly not of the same flavour; real-life problems are rarely clear-cut and so are not easy to represent using logic alone. It comes as no surprise, therefore, that computer systems based on ideas taken directly from logic have failings when applied to real-life situations. In many cases common-sense answers to problems may be excluded simply because they are outside the closed world the computer operates in.

Many databases also function in a 'closed world'. A database on flights run by a certain airline company will list the cities between which planes fly, but not cities between which they don't. The database is forced to adopt a closed-world view of things because this is by far the most practical. The number of negative facts far exceeds the number of positive facts. To state all negative facts explicitly would not be practical.

See also: Logic programming, Explicit v. tacit knowledge, Default reasoning

COMBINATIONAL
EXPLOSION

Search

This refers to the way the complexity of problems seems to explode as
the problems get bigger. Combinatorial explosion is a general term to describe how the number of combinations of things increases enormously as

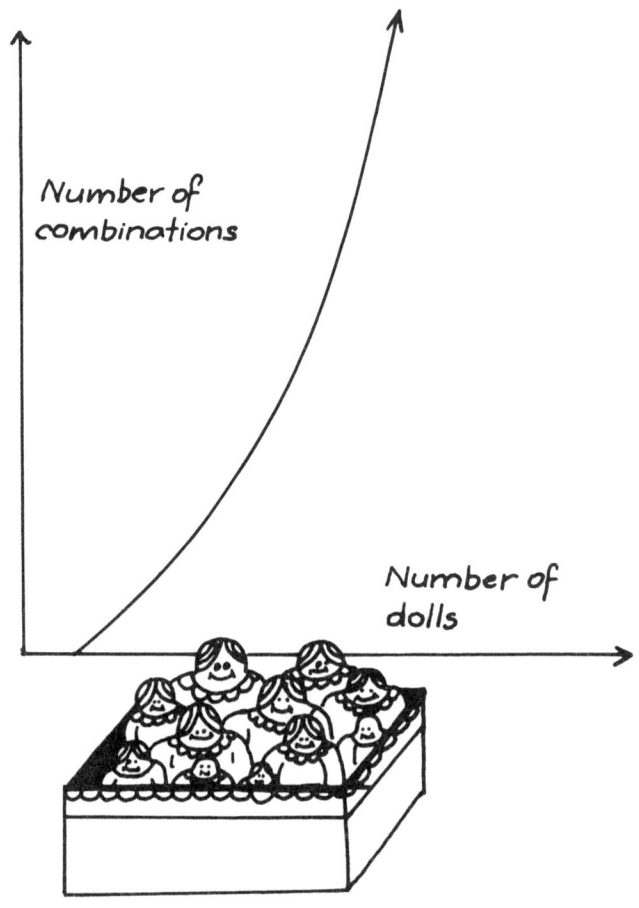

the number of those things increases a bit. For example, suppose you were trying to make a Russian doll set by picking five dolls out of a box at random. The more Russian dolls in the box, the more combinations there are and the longer it takes to find a group of five dolls which fit inside each other in the right way. This problem suffers from the combinatorial explosion: the number of possible sets shoots up as you add more dolls to the box.

The *travelling salesman problem* is one that explodes in complexity like this as the problem size expands.

Problems which run up against the combinatorial explosion cannot be solved by searching all possible solutions for the best one, so various approaches (heuristics, rules, pruning) have to be used to try to reduce the number of options to be tried.

The *Lighthill Report* on AI in Britain said that, while existing programs worked well on simple problems, they were likely to run up against the combinatorial explosion when they were applied to real-world complexity. Consequently they were poor models for intelligence.

See also: Algorithm, NP

COMPILED KNOWLEDGE

Theory/
Philosophy

Compiled knowledge is working knowledge into which much deeper knowledge has been distilled, producing some 'rules of thumb'. It is the sort of knowledge that you are taught in elementary school. For example, in biology, your teacher might tell you that two white mice will always have white mouse offspring. This is a considerable simplification of what the teacher knows, but is a good enough rule of thumb for most mouse-breeders. By contrast, the teacher knows why white mice have white offspring, involving knowledge of a range of biological and biochemical facts. This knowledge is much harder to learn, because there is more of it, but it can be applied to a range of other situations as well, and so could be more useful.

Compiled knowledge is often the most appropriate for knowledge-based systems, as it can greatly reduce both the amount of information the system must hold and the amount of reasoning it must do on that information.

Related terms are *shallow* and *deep knowledge*, again roughly meaning 'rule of thumb' and 'understanding of fundamental causes', respectively. It is not clear how useful deep knowledge is to everyday life. Studies of scientists show that they often use shallow knowledge even if they have deep knowledge about the domain concerned, because shallow knowledge works just as well. For example, in the eighteenth century an explanation of the murine family above would mention germinal particles in the blood, or the immanent mouse in the father's sperm, and say nothing about DNA at all. However, white mice still had white offspring. Thus all three ways are successful in describing how white mice have white offspring. So there is some debate about whether deep knowledge is a substantially more effective way of describing the world than shallow knowledge.

See also: Explicit v. tacit knowledge

46

COMPILER

General
computer
term

A compiler is a program which translates one language – usually a high-level computer language like Fortran or Cobol – into machine instructions, in a fashion which exactly preserves the meaning of the program. The machine-code version is sometimes also called *executable code*. Languages which are usually translated for the computer by compilers include Fortran, Pascal and C.

Traditionally, a compiler takes the whole program and translates it into machine code. If the program has a mistake in it, you have to go back to the original program (*source code*) and correct it, and then compile again. This is the process of debugging. (This contrasts with *interpreters*, which translate each instruction as they come across it.) The advantage of translating using a compiler is that the resulting machine-code program runs faster than an interpreted program.

AI has blurred the distinction between compilers and interpreters by generating hybrid compiler-interpreters, such as that used with the language SmallTalk. Thus SmallTalk is fast and makes programs easy to debug. Some such systems compile programs incrementally, that is, translating them into intermediate levels which are faster to interpret than the original language would be, but are easier to debug than the machine code.

See also: Interpreter

COMPUTER AIDED INSTRUCTION

Theory/
Philosophy

Computers have been used in three ways to aid teaching. There have been computer languages and environments specifically aimed at instruction, usually of computer programming: Seymour Papert's Logo is a well-known example. There have been programs which are designed to simulate something which is to be learned which cannot be done in the classroom: astronautics or genetics might be examples here. The programs are meant as simulation programs; learning is a side-effect. The third category is the only one in which AI has a significant role: it is intelligent CAI (ICAI), in which the 'intelligence' is used to find out where the student requires coaching, and to direct the session accordingly.

Early attempts, more computer-aided learning (CAL) than true ICAI, were frame-orientated. A template problem would be stated, and all the possible answers anticipated. Thus the question '2 + 3 =?' might be posed, and responses for < 4, 5, 6 and > 6 provided. In this case the 'intelligence' is pre-programmed.

Later programs used AI techniques to determine why the student had given a wrong answer. This requires an internal representation of both the knowledge area to be learned and the student's knowledge of that area. This latter could include knowledge about the student's beliefs and certainties about the knowledge. A wide range of techniques have been used to re-present both types of knowledge. In the late 1970s rules about teaching methods (as opposed to rules about the subject area) were introduced to guide the program, more closely modelling what a human teacher might do. This area is still rather rudimentary.

ICAI programs have to deal with students' learning problems, but also with the language they use (natural language) and with the informality of reasoning present in many areas. People often describe even quite formal areas of learning, like mathematics, in informal language. So any program attempting to tutor (as EXCHECK does in mathematical logic) must adapt formal internal representations of the knowledge to less formal ones suitable for mere human understanding. ICAI programs generate their own problems to set the student (rather than having a pre-programmed repertoire). They also analyse the answers not only to see if they are correct but also to modify future problems so as to focus on the student's weakpoints, using pattern recognition or inductive-learning techniques to find out the student's knowledge (or belief) about the subject. The program can assume that the student has a subset of the program's knowledge, or can assume that he has a flawed version of all the knowledge (or both). The latter is related to debugging in automatic programming, since a student who has flawed knowledge about some area can be thought of as similar to a program which processes information about that area, but which has a bug in it.

See also: Frame, Script

CONCURRENCY

General
computer
term

This means having two or more things going on at once on your computer. For example, for most microcomputer systems the printer can run concurrently with the computer, so that while the printer is printing out a page the computer is preparing the next one. This, then, is a term for parallel processing, but one usually reserved for systems in which relatively autonomous sections perform quite different tasks (such as printing v. computing v. reading from a disk). Large computers running time-sharing systems can simulate a lot of smaller computers running concurrently: although there is only one computer there, the users all feel that they have the computer to themselves. This illusion breaks down if hundreds of people are using it because then each user only gets a tiny fraction of a computer to play with and the computer's response to commands slows as the number of users (processes) increases.

See also: Parallel processing, Process

CONNECTIONISM

Neural nets

Connectionism is the study of a type of neural net called a 'connectionist net'. Connectionist nets and connectionism are sometimes effectively synonyms for neural nets. (This is not strictly correct. Connectionism is the study of computational systems where the connections between simple elements are critical to the processing performed by the system. Neural networks are networks of elements which behave in a manner similar to nerve cells. Real nerve cells, for example, can do quite a bit of processing in their own right.)

1. The processing elements of the networks ('neurones') have only a small number of states, i.e. they have only a very small memory. (By comparison, a mircocomputer has a vast number of internal states, corresponding to each of the different things that can be stored in its memory.)
2. The neurones are linked by any number of connections to other elements. These can be activating or inhibiting connections: activating connections add to the chance that the target neurone will in turn 'fire', while inhibiting ones reduce the chance.
3. The connections carry no coded information.

Information is coded according to which connections exist between elements of the net, not by the messages passing along them or by the memory states of the elements themselves: hence the name 'connectionism'. This means that it can be hard to decode the network's output, so nets can be arranged so that a particular connection (arising from a particular neurone) signals a specific result or concept.

Connectionist networks have several properties which may make them potentially more efficient than more conventional computers at some tasks. Among these tasks are the following.

1. *Learning.* Using *back propagation* and recirculation methods, connectionist networks can learn very rapidly.
2. *Stability and robustness.* Slightly altering either the input to or the output from an element of the network only alters the whole network's output slightly.
3. *Rapid convergence.* Connectionist networks can come up with solutions to some problems very quickly where conventional computers are very slow. Such problems typically have huge numbers of potential solutions, and are highly interconnected, so a decision about the solution to one part of the problem can affect many other parts. Typical of such problems are the *task assignment* and *travelling salesman* problems.

Connectionist networks are types of neural net, and as such are amenable to modelling on a parallel computer. In the absence of parallel hardware there are several software simulations available for microcomputers. A few connectionist networks have been built as hardware (as opposed to software simulations): the Silicon Retina and the image classification machine WIZARD are examples.

As film titles would have it, connectionist nets are 'based on an idea by' biological neural nets. Many neural-net simulations could be viewed as entirely conventional programs for manipulating matrices, the net being represented as an array of boxes representing all the possible connections between the neurons which are filled with numbers representing the connection's actual strength. This emphasizes the importance of the connection network, rather than the detail of how you draw a picture of it.

See also: Neural net, Hopfield net, Silicon Retina

CONNECTION MACHINE

Hardware

A commercially available parallel computer invented by Danny Hillis, the Connection Machine has 65 536 processors (64K) connected up in a hypercube configuration. It is an MIMD (multiple instruction, multiple data) machine, i.e. each of the processors can be doing something different from its neighbours at any one time. Relatively small processors (they have only 512 bytes of memory each) can operate together much faster than the fastest conventional computer. The programmer can define how the processors are going to be connected up: hence the name, which emphasizes not merely large numbers of processors but also the ability to join them up in any combination to solve a problem. This flexibility and massive parallelism makes the Connection Machine well suited to software simulations of a range of connectionist networks, although the Connection Machine is not a neural net.

See also: Parallel processing

COOPERATIVE SYSTEM

Expert
systems

The term 'cooperative system' is used mainly in the field of expert-system technology. Broadly speaking, it refers to an ideal system of the future which offers an interface carefully designed to suit the user's needs. Such a system would work closely and interactively with the user.

To understand this vision better, imagine consulting a computerized *Yellow Pages*. The dialogue between you and the system might be as follows.

You: Are there any plumbers in my area on 24-hour call?

Computer: Yes, there are 30. Shall I list them?

You: Are there any that specialize in blocked drain-pipes?

Computer: Mr Jones (tel. 56087) advertises 'blocked drains'. However, he operates from ten miles away. Blocked drain-pipes are a separate category in the *Yellow Pages*. Under 'drain, sewer and pipe cleaning', the following companies offer a 24-hour service in your area:

Sweet Drains tel. 333409
Unblockit Gang tel. 378409

The cooperative system, then, should have a model of what is important to the user and anticipate his or her needs. It should also be able to reason in a simple way, and refer to concepts and terminology that the user understands.

To design such a cooperative system requires a good understanding of how people interact with experts and what to expect from a consultation. Cognitive psychologists, who are interested in how people think and reason, are therefore playing an important part in cooperative system research.

See also: Human-factors research

54

CYBERNETICS

Theory/
Philosophy

Cybernetics was developed by Norbert Weiner in the 1940s as the theory of control and communication common to machines and biological systems. Thus it was used to describe how animals controlled their limbs, and how machines could carry out analogous functions.

The study of cybernetics in society is now regarded as sociology: that in biological systems has been absorbed into ecology, physiology and cognitive science, with only the latter being regarded as directly relevant to AI. Thus cybernetics in its narrower, modern sense means control of and communication with machines, especially robots. In particular, it studies the 'feedback' mechanisms by which a machine keeps track of what it is doing. Feedback is a key concept in control. A feedback mechanism is one in which the result of an operation is used to control that operation. For example, the speedometer of a car (measuring how fast it is going) might be connected to its accelerator (controlling how fast it is going). Negative feedback occurs when an increase in output causes a decrease in input – if the car speeds up, the system eases up on the gas – and is a classic 'stabilizing' mechanism. Positive feedback occurs when an increase in output causes an increase in input.

DARPA

Funding

The Defense Advanced Research Projects Agency is a US agency, sponsored by the Department of Defense, that looks into pure research topics of long-term relevance to defence problems. DARPA commissions studies of specific areas, funds research and maintains specific research facilities such as the ARPANET electronic-mail network. Among the areas DARPA has supported are speech recognition, neural nets, expert systems and a range of vision programmes.

See also: ESPRIT, Fifth-generation projects

DATAFLOW

General
computer
term

Dataflow is a way of analysing or solving problems so as to emphasize which bits of the problem depend on the data generated by which other bits. In a standard computer, the choice of which instruction is to be executed next depends on which was executed last. In a dataflow machine, the choice is made to depend on the data available for processing. The instructions are 'triggered' by the availability of the items on which they operate, not by the order of the instructions in the logical flow of the program.

Because in any computation several items of data may be ready to be processed at once, dataflow languages are well suited in theory to parallel-processing methods, with several processors processing several items of data at the same time. However, in practice, large problems are hard to solve using dataflow methods, as the amount of communication needed rises steeply with the number of dataflow processors, and so takes a larger and larger fraction of the overall processing time.

See also: Parallel processing

DECLARATIVE PROGRAMMING LANGUAGE

Prog.
techniques

In a declarative programming language, the programmer specifies a number of 'assertions', or facts, from which the system can infer other facts in a logical manner. A declarative program might, for example, consist of facts written in the following form.

A and B are a type of C
A likes B
A has the characteristics B, C and D
A is true if B, C and D are true

A major class of declarative languages is *functional* or *applicative* languages: for example, ML, Hope and Miranda.

See also: Knowledge base, Prolog

58

DEDUCTION

Theory/
Philosophy

Deduction is defined as 'logically correct inference', which means that it is the way of deriving inescapable conclusions from various starting statements. The rules say that you can shuffle about what you know but cannot assume anything else. The starting statements are called axioms, or, if they are in a computer, formulae, assertions, or entries in a knowledge base or database. Generally, deduction involves making general statements more specific, and comes in two flavours:

1. *Modus ponens*
   Axiom: If I am eating chips then I am happy
   Axiom: I am eating chips
   Conclusion: Therefore I am happy
   [Given that A implies B, and given A, we conclude B.]
2. *Modus tollens*
   Axiom: If I am eating spinach I am unhappy.
   Axiom: I am not unhappy
   Conclusion: Therefore I am not eating spinach
   [Given that A implies B, and given not B, we conclude not A.]

Deduction is the category of logic on which *predicate calculus* is based. Because it works surely and predictably, it is also the basis for logic programming languages like *Prolog*, although Prolog does not implement all of classical logic.

See also: Propositional calculus

DEFAULT REASONING

General AI
term

The term 'default reasoning' is used to describe certain forms of computer inference which do not adhere strictly to classical logic.

Many AI systems employ logic to reason about the facts and rules they possess. Although such systems will always be logically correct, they operate in a closed world: they 'know' a very limited number of facts and can only manipulate these using the laws of logic they have been given.

For systems that deal with real-world concepts, pure logic in unadulterated form is often inappropriate. Some conclusions make obvious (common) sense, although, from a logical point of view, they are unjustified. Default reasoning allows you to generalize that certain things are likely to be true, simply for the sake of argument. For example, suppose you have a database on cars. You might use the following rule.

Runs on petrol if not runs on diesel.

This means that if the database does not show explicitly that a car runs on diesel, then you can generally say that it runs on petrol, although your argument is not logically sound.

See also: Closed-world assumption

DELIVERY SYSTEM

General
computer
term

A delivery system consists of the basic elements of software and hardware needed to run a particular computer program. Contrast a delivery system to a development environment which includes an editor, debugging facilities, compilers and other components needed to write the software as well as to run it.

'Delivery system' is another term for *run-time system*. If you are a customer who simply wants to use the software and has no intention of changing and developing it further, then a delivery system is the cheaper option. Not only is the software itself less expensive, but a delivery system will usually run on a cheaper computer, for example an ordinary PC. The full development environment, however, may need a technical workstation.

DEPTH

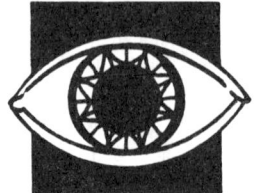

Vision

In vision or robotics, depth is the measure of how far away from the camera or robot something is. Depth is determined from machine inputs by one of several methods:

1. *Stereopsis* (Figure a). This is the method our eyes use over short distances, as do some range-finders. Two images of the same scene are taken by two cameras at slightly different positions, and the depth of objects in the field is deduced from differences in the pictures.
2. *Occultation* (Figure b). This entails seeing that Fred is half-hidden by Charlie, and so knowing that Fred must be behind Charlie. This pre-supposes that we know what Fred's shape is so that we can detect when some of him is missing. We also need to know what shape Fred is from a range of different directions.
3. *Size cues*. This method is based on the fact that things further away look smaller. If you know what the absolute size of something is, then you can work out how far away it is from the size of its image. This is also difficult to implement for anything other than small sets of standard shapes.
4. *Radar*. This, and other echo systems like sonar, can give a direct meas-urement of distance (after suitable electronic processing). These approaches are reliable, and consequently are used in robotics.

Many of these systems require the computer to have a substantial know-ledge base about the actual shape of objects, so as to deduce what the images are images of. Thus they are much easier to implement in very simple environments like *blocks world* (or physical versions of them in which the only objects in view are of a few well-defined shapes) where the number of items that could be in view is very small, than in the real world.

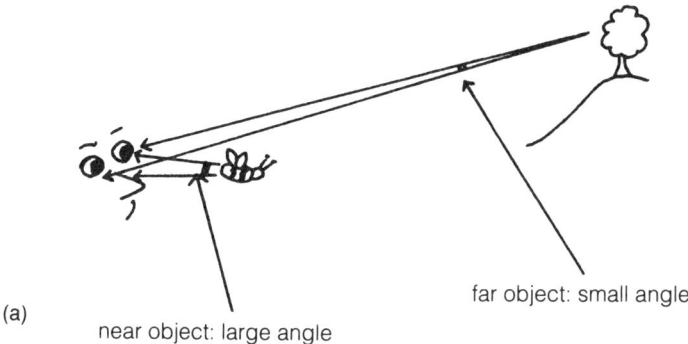

(a)

far object: small angle

near object: large angle

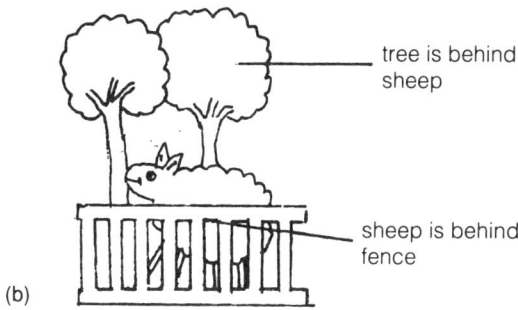

tree is behind sheep

sheep is behind fence

(b)

Depth information is used to turn a 2D sketch, a flat pictorial repres-entation in a computer vision system, into a *2 ¹/₂D sketch*, in which the distance from the camera of every object in view is shown.

See also: 2 ¹/₂D sketch

DEPTH FIRST SEARCH

Search

Many problems can be represented, for the purpose of computerization, as a search tree. This representation shows the stages in searching for the answer to the problem as a number of 'nodes'. Lines between nodes often symbolize 'operators'. These are procedures or actions which have been applied to move from one stage in solving the problem to another.

Depth-first and *breadth-first search* are two techniques for searching methodically through nodes in a search tree. To illustrate what is involved in depth-first search, consider a computer wanting to get from San Francisco to Nice in France by plane.

A search tree gives a representation of the routes the computer knows are possible, as shown opposite.

The search through this tree is shown as depth first, left to right. The computer investigates 'blindly' one town after another in a methodical fashion until it encounters a solution. Nodes currently under investigation are put on a 'stack' in computer memory, are tested to see if they give a useful solution to the problem, and then are 'popped' off the stack if they fail to yield a useful result.

The advantage of depth-first search over breadth-first search is, in part, that only a limited number of nodes are held in memory at once.

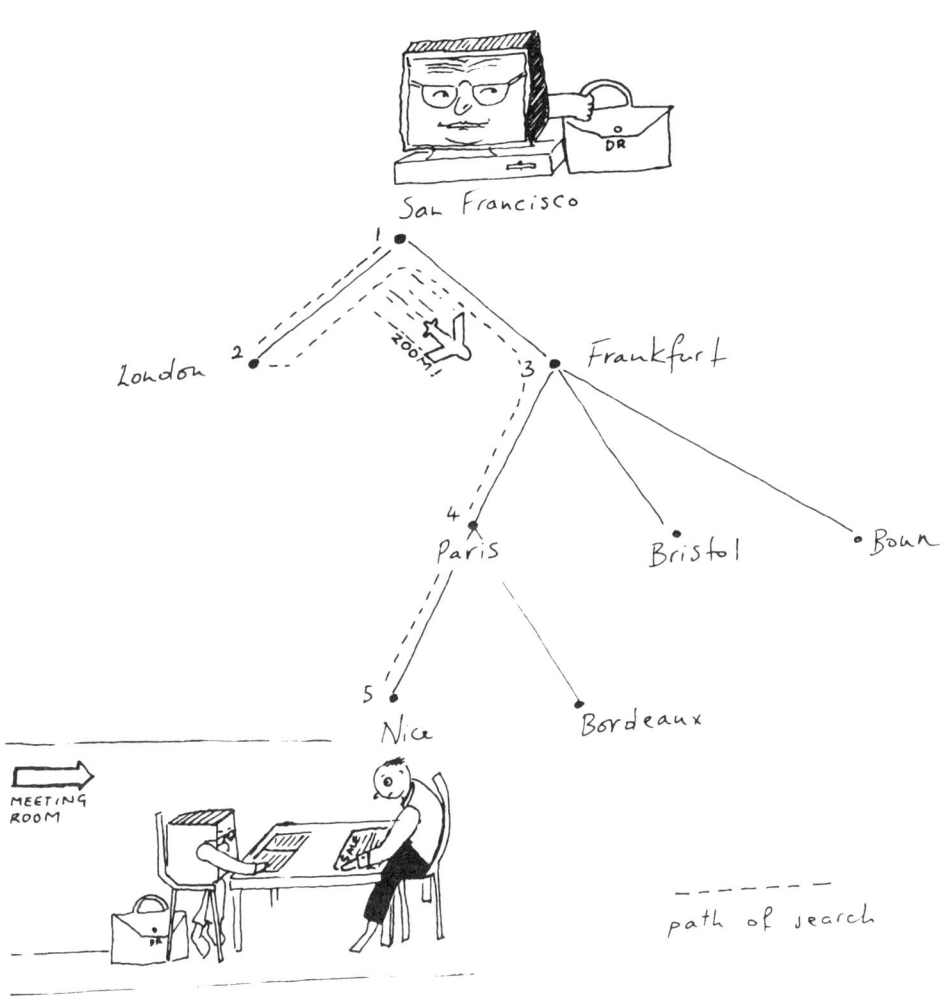

San Francisco

1

2 London

ZOOM!

3 Frankfurt

4 Paris

Bristol

Bonn

5 Nice

Bordeaux

MEETING ROOM

path of search

65

DERIVATION TREE

NLP

Grammars are sometimes represented as diagrams called 'derivation trees'. The derivation tree below shows the structure of the sentence 'Eleanor gave the sandwich to Thomas'. Note the following terminology which is used in discussing such representations.

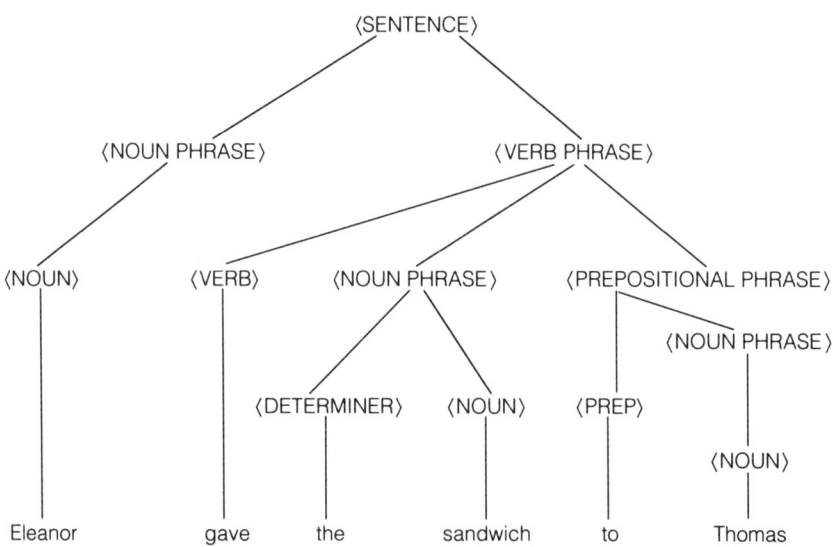

1. *Non-terminal symbols* include all those symbols which are not at the tips of the branches of the tree. These are the symbols denoted in the re-write rules by angled brackets and which can be redefined in terms of other symbols.

2. *Terminal symbols* are those that cannot be redefined further: they are at the leaves of the tree – for example, 'Eleanor' and 'gave'.

See also: Grammar, Parser

DEVELOPMENT ENVIRONMENT

General
computer
term

An AI development environment consists of a number of development tools for the programmer to write AI applications. Some of these environments are hardware-specific; others will run on particular breeds of standard computer, PCs for example. Some common types of development environment are as follows.

1. *Prototyping tools.* These can be used to experiment with a knowledge representation or user interface before you commit yourself to the cost of a professionally engineered product. Prolog remains a sound prototyping tool: simple Prologs on the market are relatively inexpensive and usually include editing and debugging facilities, plus a method for extending the Prolog code you write into C.
2. *Expert-system shells.* These provide a selection of programming tools – a knowledge-representation language, an editor, an inference engine and so on – for writing expert systems.
3. *Toolkits.* These provide extensive facilities for the development of larger, more elaborate, expert systems. Toolkits typically include a wide range of integrated programming techniques including logic programming, object-orientated programming, the use of production rules and also conventional programming languages. The inference engine may be able to use information from large databases held on another computer system across a network.

See also: Rapid prototyping, Expert-system shell

DEVELOPMENT TOOL

General
computer
term

A development tool is a piece of software designed to turn the development of AI systems into a more manageable task. Development tools are sold as a development environment comprising a selection of development tools.

Common development tools are as follows:

1. *Programming languages.* You might be supplied with Prolog, Lisp, some form of C, Poplog and so on. A compiler or interpreter to convert programs to a usable form is also needed.
2. *Editing facilities.* These enable the programmer to write, erase or alter parts of a program. Interactive debugging, allowing the programmer to list the program in one part of the screen and control its compilation or interpretation in another, is provided with the more sophisticated environments.
3. *A knowledge-representation language.* This allows the programmer to formalize knowledge about the domain as a set of rules or other formalism.

See also: Rapid prototyping, Experimental system

DISTRIBUTED PROCESSING

Hardware

Distributed processing is computation carried out by more than one computer at once. It is therefore a form of parallel processing. The key distinction which makes some parallel processing applications into distributed processing is that the computation is distributed among a number of processors which may be doing rather different things. Thus the processors tend to be fairly complex parts of the whole which can perform programs in their own right. The simplest processor found in a distributed-processing computer is probably that found in the *Connection Machine*. The most complex can be an entire mainframe computer, as exemplified by a recent experiment where a huge mathematical calculation (factoring a 100-digit number) was performed by 400 separate computers in the USA.

Distributed processors are a specific type of network. However, not all networks are distributed processors. The main difference is that distributed processing is transparent to the user, i.e. the user of one element of a distributed processor does not have to worry about how to connect his element to the others.

Just as distributed processing is a special kind of network, so parallel processing is a special kind of distributed processing, in that the processors themselves are usually identical, and (in SIMD (single instruction, multiple data) machines), carry out identical instructions.

Neural networks are also distributed processors in a different sense. It is not possible to say *which* neuron in a neural network is doing any part of a computation, as the computation is not described with an algorithm consisting of separate bits. Rather, the whole network has an activity which represents the progress of the computation, without there being one neuron we can point to as performing any one basic operation. Thus as well as distributing our program across a lot of processors, we distribute the basis of the computation itself.

See also: Neural nets, Parallel processing

DOMAIN

General
computer
term

1. A domain is an area of knowledge or expertise to which AI techniques may be applied. For example, you might apply expert-system technology to the domain of oil drilling, or a search technique to the domain of chess.
2. The domain of a function is the set of values to which it may be applied. For example:

'odd 3' is true;
'odd 6' is false;
'odd ("hello")' is a type error.

The function 'odd' has the domain integers and the range {true, false}.

EDGE DETECTION

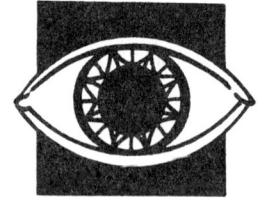

Vision

This is the computer-vision process of finding sharp changes in darkness or lightness in a picture, which are usually caused by the edges of objects in the view. The real world has relatively few things painted black with sharp edges resting on a white background, so images have to be processed before edges can be extracted from them. Thus pictures of faces, for example, are contrast-enhanced into Warhol-like cartoons with lots of contrasting edges, and often reduced to a black-and-white only image (*binary image*).

The method is to look at the change of lightness or darkness across an image, and search for zero crossings (ZCs), i.e. places where the amount of light goes from positive (bright) to negative (dark). Wherever a ZC occurs, the brightness of the image is changing at a maximum rate from light to dark or dark to light, and so here is a good candidate for an 'edge'.

The neural nets in the retina of the eye also perform edge detection, as an early part of the detection of shapes by animals.

See also: Primal sketch

ELASTIC LOGIC

Expert
systems

Elastic logic is an idea for deciding which rules in a knowledge base should be used on a particular occasion. It has been suggested for expert-system applications.

The usefulness of elastic logic is that it allows an expert system to incorporate potentially incompatible expertise from more than one source. When the expert system is consulted, it uses one set of rules (obtained by interviewing human expert A) for the first minute, and then switches to using the rules derived from the expertise of expert B for the second minute. The system then reverts to using expert A's opinion for the third minute, and back again to expert B's opinion for the fourth. Thus the user is happy that the expert system is not biased, and is representative of more than one authority on the domain.

EPISTEMOLOGY

Theory/
Philosophy

Epistemology is the study of knowledge. This somewhat abstract discipline came into AI through the desire to define exactly what knowledge is before building a knowledge-based system. Epistemology asks what it means to say that a system actually knows something. For example, the word processor used to write this book contains a lot of words about AI, but does it *know* anything about the subject? Epistemology is also concerned with how knowledge is acquired, and how it can be modified by experience. Belief is an important part of epistemology, as most human knowledge is a combination of facts and beliefs about those facts.

Lastly, epistemology is a blanket term to cover the study of types of knowledge, such as tacit v. explicit, shallow v. deep.

See also: Knowledge engineering

ESPRIT

Funding

ESPRIT stands for European Strategic Research Programme in Information Technology. Funded by the EEC, the pilot phase was launched in 1983, with the main program in 1984. A follow-on program started in 1987. In part, ESPRIT grew in response to the Japanese Fifth Generation Projects initiative, which aimed to produce more useful and usable computers in the 1990s. More generally, ESPRIT was an attempt to produce a concerted effort in the field of information technology in Europe.

The ESPRIT programme involved many types of research. The advanced information processing part of the programme included a number of artificial intelligence projects, such as an expert-systems builder, means of knowledge representation, natural-language interrogation, parallel architectures and languages, knowledge-based management systems, and the use of non-monotonic reasoning techniques.

ESPRIT was followed by ESPRIT II, which was launched in December 1987 and included the application of knowledge-based techniques to design; knowledge engineering; advanced system architectures and robotics. This too has now been succeeded, by ESPRIT III which will spend about £570 million and will run until 1994.

See also: Fifth-generation projects

EXPERIMENTAL SYSTEM

General
computer
term

An experimental system is one pieced together in the laboratory to demonstrate a principle or approach to a problem.

The next step in the development path is the *prototype* (which does what the final, released model is meant to do under ideal conditions), and the *pilot version* (which is the version released for beta testing to see if it will work in the real world). In practice the boundaries between these stages are rather blurred.

See also: Rapid prototyping

EXPERT SYSTEMS

Expert
systems

Expert systems are amongst the more commercially visible manifestations of artificial intelligence. An expert system is a program which embodies 'expertise' about something and which allows the user to ask the computer certain questions about that expertise. The expertise is always in a very restricted area of knowledge called the *domain*.

One of the first domains to be tackled in a commercial expert system was the configuration of orders for large computer systems. A large computer installation has so many components that ordering the right ones can be exceedingly complicated. To help its salesmen sell the right thing to the right customer, the computer company Digital developed an expert system called XCON. Also known as R1, this expert system was the first of its kind, and has helped salesmen configure orders for VAX computers since 1980.

Another landmark in the history of expert-system technology was MYCIN. Developed by Edward Shortcliff of Stanford University in the 1970s, MYCIN diagnosed bacterial infections of the blood by discussing certain characteristics of the bacterium with the user. MYCIN, in common with other famous expert systems (see Appendix A) is based on a formalism called a *production rule*, a rule of an IF...THEN format:

IF shape is round and colour is green THEN name is apple.

Although many expert systems are still based on this type of rule, many other representations of knowledge are now used (see *object-orientated programming*, *frames* and *scripts*).

The process of turning an expert's *knowledge* into a computer system is far from easy. Bear in mind that a serious expert system may take several man-years to construct. It is not the coding (the writing of the computer program itself) which takes so long, it is the process of extracting expertise from the human expert and then thinking of a useful way to present it to the user. These points are explained under *knowledge engineering* and *knowledge acquisition*.

In the 1970s, many expert systems handled uncertain information. The usual technique was to express a degree of implication artificially as a scalar value: 'It's going to rain, certainty 0.8' or 'there's a probability of 0.6 that this information is right'. Where the system had to assimilate many uncertain statements at once and produce some new piece of information, complex numerical methods or 'calculi' were used. Amongst the better-known examples are:

1. Bayes' theorem, which was used in the expert system PROSPECTOR;
2. the Dempsey-Shafer theory;
3. evidential reasoning;
4. confirmation theory, which used to calculate the certainty factors used by the expert system MYCIN. The certainty factor of a given hypothesis is the difference between a measure that the hypothesis is true, and a measure that the hypothesis is refuted.

There are various problems with these numerical methods. By and large, calculi are *ad hoc* methods: for a given domain, it is often not known what the probability distribution of a particular occurrence is. Furthermore, it is very hard to take into account how the occurrence of one thing affects the occurrence of others. It may not even be explicitly known how, or even if, facts are dependent.

Perhaps equally important is the fact that it is unnatural for either experts or users to specify the degree of truth of statements with such numerical precision. An expert finds it hard to give a probability value for every piece of expertise he has. By and large, calculi offer a limited way of handling the kind of reasoning used by humans.

In the 1980s, uncertainty began to be handled by adding more knowledge about the domain, with more rules to specify the expertise. A completely different approach is potentially possible using *neural nets*, where competing possibilities vie simultaneously for dominance. However, although neural networks provide a way of handling uncertainty, when it comes to explaining their reasoning in arriving at a conclusion, conventional approaches do much better.

The components of an expert system are summarized in the diagram opposite. Each component receives an entry entirely devoted to it in this book, to which you should refer for greater detail.

There are many types of expert system currently in use. They include the following.

The components of an expert system

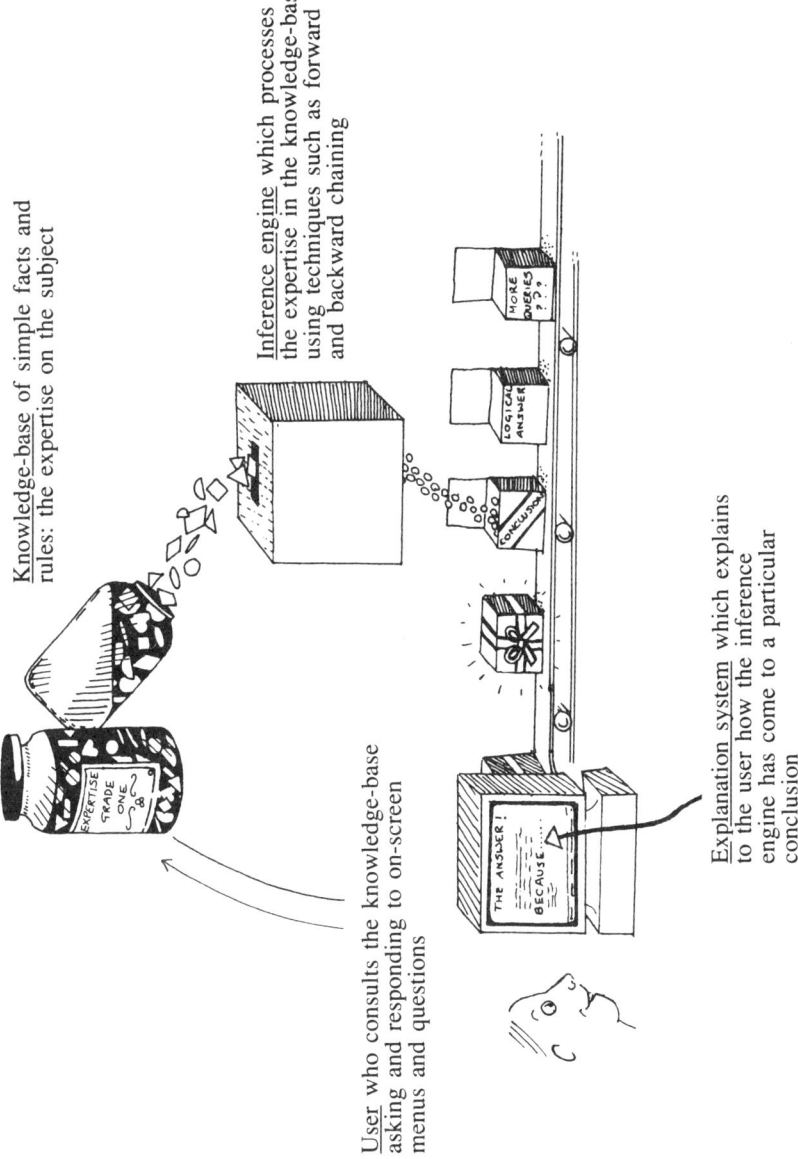

Knowledge-base of simple facts and
rules: the expertise on the subject

Inference engine which processes
the expertise in the knowledge-base
using techniques such as forward
and backward chaining

User who consults the knowledge-base
asking and responding to on-screen
menus and questions

Explanation system which explains
to the user how the inference
engine has come to a particular
conclusion

1. *Advisory systems.* These are used to represent policies and procedures in areas such as personnel management, taxation, and pension schemes. The user writes a series of questions and is then given advice about a procedure or policy in the form of customized text on the screen.

2. *Clerical checking systems.* These are rule-based systems which do simple checks on incoming information being processed by Accounts, Order Processing or other clerical departments. An expert system might be used to check, for a certain product, that the options ordered are consistent with that product. In the case of, say, a power drill, the expert system would check that the manual and cable supplied with it were suitable for the country to which the tool was being sent.

3. *Ordering and configuring systems.* These expert systems take descriptive information direct from the non-technical customer or salesman describing what they want a certain product to do, and convert this information into a list of orderable components that will be needed to do the job. For example, the salesman might specify the number of workstations, the software they need to run, the communications facilities needed and so on. The expert system would respond by telling the salesman which cables, disk drives, tape drives and screens to order, and which system software was needed.

4. *Real-time monitoring systems.* Real-time monitoring systems continuously monitor many variables at once and make adjustments accordingly. Examples are in medical monitoring where the expert system monitors the patient's physiological processes, and in industry where the system monitors a manufacturing process.

5. *Battlefield systems.* These systems receive large quantities of low-level data (via radar or radio about the position and type of aircraft, for example) from which they build a meaningful model of what is going on. The mass of data received is thus rendered in a form easier to understand for humans involved in tactical decisions. Such systems are fallible, of course: data can be misinterpreted.

See also: Certainty, Inference engine, Backward chaining, Forward chaining, Explanation system, Elastic logic, Expert-system shell

EXPERT SYSTEM SHELL

Expert
systems

An expert-system shell is an applications package designed for constructing an expert system. Although it is possible to write an expert system from scratch using a programming language, this may be unnecessary. An expert-system shell provides ready-built tools for constructing simple expert systems, for appropriate domains.

What does an expert-system shell provide? First and foremost, it provides the programmer with a means for representing knowledge. There are many techniques for doing this, the best known being the *production rule*, adopted in part because it is one of the most 'natural' representations to the less technical, the rules being written in something approaching ordinary (human) language.

For example:

IF: order large
        and customer major account
        and customer not Jones and co.

THEN: discount 10%

Combining several production rules to build an expert system is, of course, quite a different matter from writing them individually. Getting even, say, 50 rules to interact properly is very tricky. You need a good understanding of the way the system will use the rules to come to conclusions, and a clear idea of the expertise you wish to encapsulate (see *knowledge engineering*).

Rules are not the only way of representing knowledge. The more sophisticated expert-system shells (or 'toolkits') provide the programmer with other methods (see *Object-oriented programming, Frame, Script*).

Once you have written the rules for an expert system, you need a program to convert them into a form the computer can actually run. For example, the rules may first need to be converted into Prolog and then compiled into executable computer code. This means that the expert system shell usually includes a *compiler* or *interpreter*, whichever is appropriate.

The part of the system which actually uses the rules to come to conclusions is the inference engine. Without an inference engine, the expert system cannot use what it knows in an 'intelligent' way. Thus an inference engine is included when you buy a shell. See *inference engine* for more detail.

In most cases, the inference engine will provide some sort of account of which rules it used when coming to a particular conclusion so that the behaviour of the expert system can be analysed. This idea is discussed under *explanation system.*

See also: Explanation system, Expert system

EXPLANATION SYSTEM

Expert
systems

An explanation system is a facility offered by an expert system to explain its reasoning. In general, today's explanation systems are based on *trace information* which shows which rules have fired and when, during the course of a consultation with the expert system. In other words, most explanation facilities base their explanation on following closely how the inference system works.

Unfortunately, trace information may be pretty unintelligible and not really what the user hopes for. After all, if you consulted a human expert on chemistry and wanted to know his reasoning behind a certain conclusion, you would expect a model you understood with useful metaphors and reference points. Information like this:

by rule 31 T = 34.6
and SU conc 56 = TRUE
implication barium prec and calcium (0.7) & undetermined

is not quite what you would expect. In fact some of the more serious expert systems do a bit better than this, offering explanations somewhat closer to English. However, probing the system more carefully and asking the sort of questions you might ask a human expert is still something of the future.

With better explanation facilities in mind, researchers are examining more closely the kind of dialogue which exists between human experts and those consulting them. Within the next decade or so, more cooperative systems may be developed.

See also: Cooperative system

EXPLICIT V TACIT KNOWLEDGE

Theory/
Philosophy

Explicit knowledge is knowledge which is stated, as opposed to *tacit* or *implicit knowledge* which is not stated but which it is assumed the user possesses. It may be impossible to state tacit knowledge in any formal way. In designing a knowledge base it is essential to remember what knowledge is explicit and what is tacit, and what needs to be made explicit in the final system. This presupposes that we have a good model of what information we need and how it is to be manipulated. This is not easy to achieve, because behind each item of explicit knowledge lies a mass of tacit knowledge which we have picked up by living in a society where everyone shares that tacit knowledge.

For example, we are told explicitly that cod are fish that live in deep seawater. Most people have never seen a live cod, so this knowledge is transferred to them as a simple, formal rule. But we learn what a fish is largely by example, from having many people pointing to cold slimy creatures of various shapes and sizes and saying 'That's a fish'. At no time have we learned any formal definition of a fish. Although taxonomists can produce exact definitions of fish, we do not use them in everyday life. And the taxonomists' definition is itself based on classes of object (such as 'animal') which are themselves not defined, but are tacit knowledge.

In a knowledge-based system, explicit knowledge appears either as data in the database or as explicit procedures in the program; our knowledge of gravity, for example, could be formulated as arithmetic rules governing rocket trajectories. The tacit knowledge is not formally entered at all, but for the system to work it must be there. Tacit knowledge may be disguised in the reasoning in the program itself, often as default reasoning. For example, the system might suppose that everything that lives in the sea is a fish unless otherwise stated. It can also be disguised as the *closed-world assumption*.

The most common place to hide tacit knowledge is in the users. Users

need a lot of tacit knowledge to understand apparently simple statements. Thus it is much easier to make knowledge bases for experts than for non-experts, as they have a much larger base of tacit knowledge to draw on.

Quite a lot of knowledge about everyday reality is tacit knowledge. As well as having to incorporate tacit knowledge in some consistent way, knowledge engineers face the problem of finding what it is in the first place. Even the most sophisticated programs cannot winkle out the knowledge that the user cannot formulate in some suitable rule or definition, and so coding tacit knowledge falls to the programmer. A truly intelligent expert system might be able to discover tacit knowledge for itself, but current expert systems are not of this sophistication.

See also: Knowledge engineering, Closed-world assumption

FIFTH GENERATION PROJECTS

Funding

A whole family of organizations and activities has grown from the Japanese Fifth Generation Projects initiative, launched in 1981, which aimed to develop a new generation of computers making use of artificial intelligence. 'Fifth generation' refers to the development of computers in steps or generations from the first (thermionic valves), though the second (discrete transistors and ferrite core memory), third (integrated circuits) and fourth (VLSI circuits handling 32- or 64-bit data).

The fifth generation of computers remains as yet unbuilt. The vision involves a computer that is natural to use, that has a good understanding of normal human language, and is capable of a high degree of human-like reasoning. The fifth generation of computers would also be able to deal with uncertainty and incomplete information.

The Japanese programme was to cover ten years and, as is usual in Japan, would be carried out by a group of large companies under the guidance of the Ministry of Trade and Industry (MITI) with a relatively small financial contribution from the government. A review of the project in 1988 showed that progress had been slower than expected; some goals would take far longer to realize than planned, and others would probably never be achieved. In particular, the prospect of developing the new knowledge bases required to enable the Fifth Generation inference machines to perform operationally, remains distant.

During 1991, the Japanese have promoted discussion of a programme to succeed the Fifth Generation. It would concentrate on neural networks with parallel computing on a large scale and has inevitably been informally called Sixth Generation.

See also: ESPRIT, ALVEY

FORWARD CHAINING

Expert
systems

Forward chaining is a method of reasoning used in expert systems. In forward chaining the computer examines the data given to it:

colour = green
shape = round
country = France

and, in the light of this information, fires certain rules:

IF: colour = green and shape = round
THEN: name of fruit is apple

Where a series of rules follow, for example:

A and B implies C
A and X implies D
A and Y implies F
C and D implies E
F and E implies Z

forward chaining causes the result of firing the first applicable rule to be handed forward. So, if A, B, E and X are true, then:

A and B implies C
A and X implies D
      ——————————→ C and D implies E
              ——————————→ F and E implies Z

This of course is a very simple example of how forward chaining can work. Real-life expert systems may use several hundred rules and use a combination of backward and forward chaining to achieve results.

See also: Backward chaining, Production rule

FRAME

Prog.
techniques

The term 'frame' was coined by Marvin Minsky in the mid-1970s. A frame is one of many methods of organizing and representing information so that it can be accessed and used methodically. A frame can be thought of as a mini-database consisting of slots containing data. Here is an example.

```
Name of frame: cakes
Specialization of: food
Type_of_cake:
    Flavours:    (chocolate, lemon puff, custard)
    Default:     chocolate
    Rules:       If brown filling then chocolate
                 If yellow filling then lemon puff
                 If white filling then custard
Size:
    Range:       (large, medium, small)
    Default:     medium
```

Characteristically, frames are hierarchically arranged, with certain named slots passed down from the parent frame to its descendants. These are 'global' slots. 'Local' slots are specific to the frame in question. In our example, all food slots inherit a global slot 'size' but the slot 'type of cake' is purely particular to the cake frame: no other frame uses it.

Frames can also contain rules concerning the use of data in the frame. The results of these rules firing can be passed to other named frames in the system.

See also: Script, Knowledge base

FRAME STORE

Hardware

This is the part of a machine vision system which takes the output of a picture detector (usually a modified TV camera) and stores it in numerical form for input into a computer. It stores several frames of the picture at a time before passing them on to the computer when required.

See also: Vision

FRONT END

General
computer
term

The 'front end' of a system is that part of it which faces the user, i.e. the sections of the program which handle input and output. In AI the program is usually a database or expert system, and can be called an *intelligent front end*. A front end which will accept a language like English from the user and translate it into some suitable code is called a *natural language front end*. Sometimes it will also translate the expert system's output into English. An example of this latter is the medical advice system ROUNDSMAN, which takes facts stored in a database of medical literature and assembles them for output into English statements. As in ROUNDSMAN, front ends can be powerful expert systems in their own right.

Front ends can also have graphical displays which help the user interact with a complicated program. The WIMP (windows, icons, mouse, pointer) input and output system, popularized by the Apple Macintosh microcomputer, is of this type.

Also referred to is a *front-end processor*. This is a piece of hardware that interfaces between a number of users, usually using disparate terminals and communication systems, and a central computer.

See also: Natural-language interface

GAME TREE

Games and
toy domains

A game tree is a representation of all the possible plays of a game. The game is of a particular sort, involving two opposing players who make alternate moves. Each player knows, at any point in the game, what the legal moves are, and what effect any move is likely to have. Unlike snakes and ladders or Ludo, which rely on chance throwing of a dice, the game must be clearly a matter of skill. The game must not involve a player hiding his hand as in a card game.

A game tree has a root node which represents the initial position of the game (see the diagram opposite). The successors of the root node are the positions the player can reach in one move. The nodes at the tips of the branches are known as the *terminal nodes*. These represent the final stages of the game, when the players can win, lose or draw.

The moves a player can make may be shown as OR nodes or AND nodes in the search tree (see *AND–OR tree*). The reason is this: when it is the player's move, he can choose which move to make. If at least one of the moves open to him leads him to a position where he is assured of a win, then, provided he is clever, a win is possible. The player can make one OR the other move to win: the node is an OR expansion.

If it is the opponent's move, the player has no choice. He can only be guaranteed to win if all the moves the opponent makes lead to positions in which the player is still assured success. The player's move has to work for each move his opponent can make. With this in mind, a node corresponding to the opponent's turn in the game is an AND expansion: he has to be able to cope with moves 1 *AND* 2.

The game tree for a sophisticated game is vast. The game of chess, for example, has about 10^{120} nodes and can never be stored and searched in any reasonable time. We have, therefore, drawn a simple game tree for noughts and crosses.

See also: Classic puzzles, AND–OR tree, Alpha-beta pruning, Chess

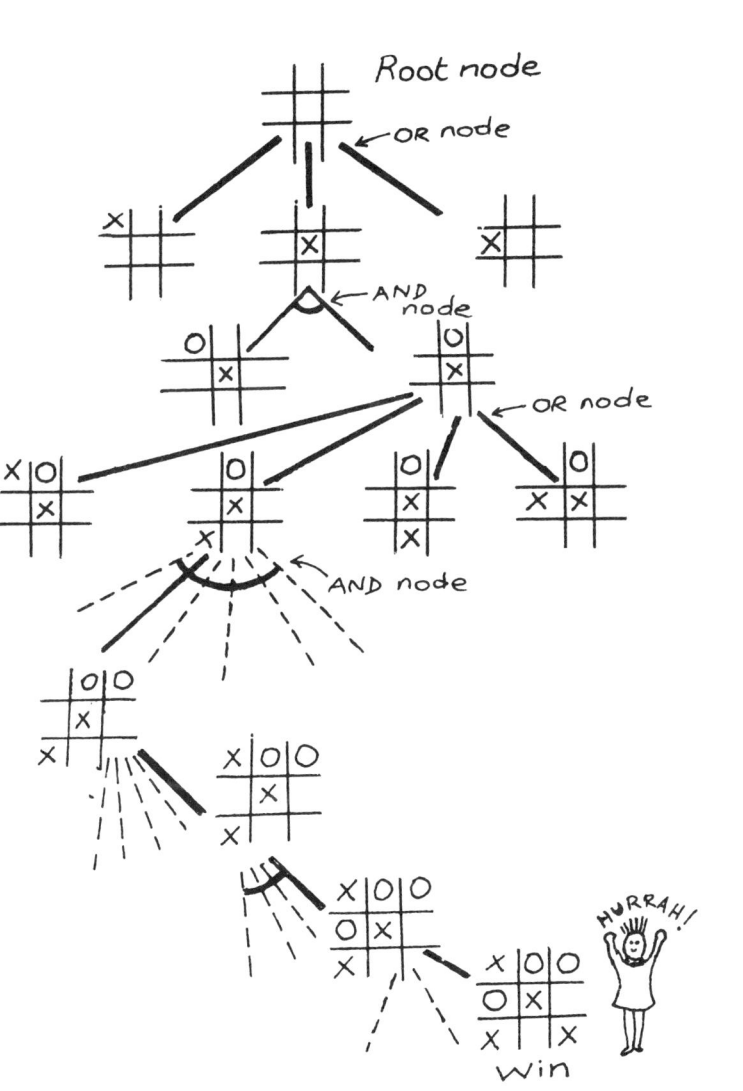

GENETIC ALGORITHM

Theory/
Philosophy

Genetic algorithms are a research topic with very few applications so far. They are a type of learning algorithm, a specific version of an empiricist algorithm which learns through trial and error. They are often used in rules-based systems of the production-rule type. Each rule has a certain associated probability. At each cycle of the program, all the rules whose left-hand sides match the actual conditions at the time are collected. Then *one* of them is 'fired'. Which one is used depends purely on chance, but the chances are biased so that rules with higher associated probabilities are fired more often. If the result of that rule firing matches the ideal solution, then the probability of its firing the next time increases. Thus after several cycles the rules that produce good answers become the ones that almost always 'fire'.

The original statement of the genetic algorithm system by John Holland enables the computer to generate new rules. These rules are inexact copies of old rules, copies with 'mutations' in them. If one of them turns out to be very good, then it will accumulate a high probability rating and so will take over from the other, older rules. Thus the computer learns to solve a problem itself even if the ideal rules to do so did not exist in its original rules set. The computer holds a schema (outline plan) of the permitted rules. Most rules are formed by recombining old ones (i.e. taking bits of different rules and splicing them together); some are formed by changing bits of a rule at random in a 'mutation'. This allows the genetic algorithm to solve problems that are intractable to hill-climbing methods, as the new combinations can 'leap' to new areas of the problem space, jumping chasms in the 'landscape' which a plodding hill-climbing algorithm cannot cross.

An interesting idea, currently being researched, is to use neural networks to implement genetic algorithms (and, conversely, to use genetic algorithms to optimize neural networks).

See also: Neural net, Automatic programming, Learning

GRAMMAR

NLP

The word 'grammar' is used in the field of natural-language processing to refer to a set of rules specifying how words may be combined into sentences.

A very simple type of grammar is the *context-free grammar*. This is one of the four basic types of grammar defined by the linguist Chomsky; it is one of the more popular types of grammar used in very simple natural-language applications, in part because it is easy to program. In this entry we use a context-free grammar to introduce some of the terminology used to describe computer grammars in general.

A context-free grammar is defined in terms of a number of *rewrite rules* or 'productions'. A rewrite rule specifies to the computer, for each basic part of speech, how it may be written in terms of simpler components. This means that, if you want to define what you mean by 'sentence', you rewrite the structure of a sentence in terms of, say, a verb phrase and a noun phrase:

<SENTENCE> ⟶ <NOUN PHRASE> <VERB PHRASE>

Then again, a noun phrase may itself be redefined, either in terms of a determiner followed by a noun, or as a determiner followed by a noun and then an adjective:

<NOUN PHRASE> ⟶ <DET> <NOUN>

<NOUN PHRASE> ⟶ <DET> <NOUN> <ADJECTIVE>

Lastly, a lexicon is used to tell the computer which English words are acceptable and what parts of speech they are.

A complete grammar for very simple sentences is given below. This grammar gives, for example:

Eleanor gave the sandwich to Thomas
Thomas kicked the orange juice to Eleanor

and equally:

sandwich gave Eleanor to Thomas

which is syntactically correct, but total nonsense semantically.

<SENTENCE> → <NOUN PHRASE> <VERB PHRASE>
<VERB PHRASE> → <VERB> <NOUN PHRASE> <PREP PHRASE>
<NOUN PHRASE> → <DET> <NOUN>
<NOUN PHRASE> → <NOUN>
<PREP PHRASE> → <PREPOSITION> <NOUN PHRASE>
<VERB> → kicked
<VERB> → gave
<PREPOSITION> → to
<NOUN> → Thomas
<NOUN> → orange juice
<NOUN> → Eleanor
<NOUN> → sandwich
<DET> → the

GREY LEVEL IMAGE

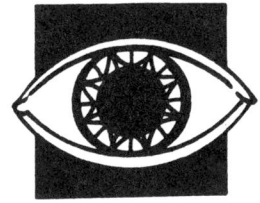

Vision

The product of the first step in computer vision, the GLI is simply a numerical description of the light intensity at each point in the picture being presented to the computer. It is a direct numerical representation of a monochrome TV image, in which the brightness of each spot on the screen is represented by a number.

See also: Binary image

HAMMING NET

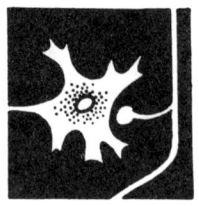

Neural nets

A type of neural net, which differs from a *Hopfield net* by the nature of the connections allowed. The net has three layers of neurons. Unlike the Hopfield net, where any neuron can connect to any other, the Hamming net is a strictly feedforward network, with input units connecting to processing units, and processing units connecting to other processing units and to output units.

Hamming nets have a substantially greater memory than Hopfield nets, and can converge on a stable pattern of activity more readily. Thus for the pattern-recognition tasks at which neural nets excel they can be an improvement.

See also: Hopfield net, Neural nets

HEURISTIC

General AI
term

A heuristic is a rule of thumb, a general principle used in reasoning. A classic heuristic is: 'people usually say they will do things much faster than they actually can'. Or, for those who can't resist mending broken clocks and barometers: 'always check for the most obvious fault first'. A heuristic is quite different from an algorithm, which is a step-wise method which always gives a precise answer. Whereas algorithms are required to be infallible, heuristics are generally right but can also lead you up the garden path if you're unlucky.

The applications of heuristics in AI are numerous. The IF...THEN rules used by many AI systems (see *production rule*) are essentially heuristics: they apply to a particular situation only, and give advice rather than a series of definite infallible instructions.

Heuristics are also used extensively to guide search. Blind search through all the possible plays of the game is obviously impractical when deciding the next move in chess. Heuristics like 'don't put your queen where it can be taken by your opponent' are needed to act as general guidelines to play. See the entries on *search* and on *chess*.

Finally, consider the use of heuristics in planning. A mathematician looking at an algebraic expression may see at once how to transform it into a simplified form. The student, however, 'does not know where to begin'. Heuristics which respond to certain recognizable patterns by recommending actions to take, can help one to decide how to proceed in a complicated problem.

See also: Knowledge base, Expert system, Algorithm, Search

HILL CLIMBING

General AI
term

This term is used to describe an approach to solving problems. Most popular in the 1960s, it is still widely used in some applications.

A hill-climbing algorithm is one that looks at the solution to a problem

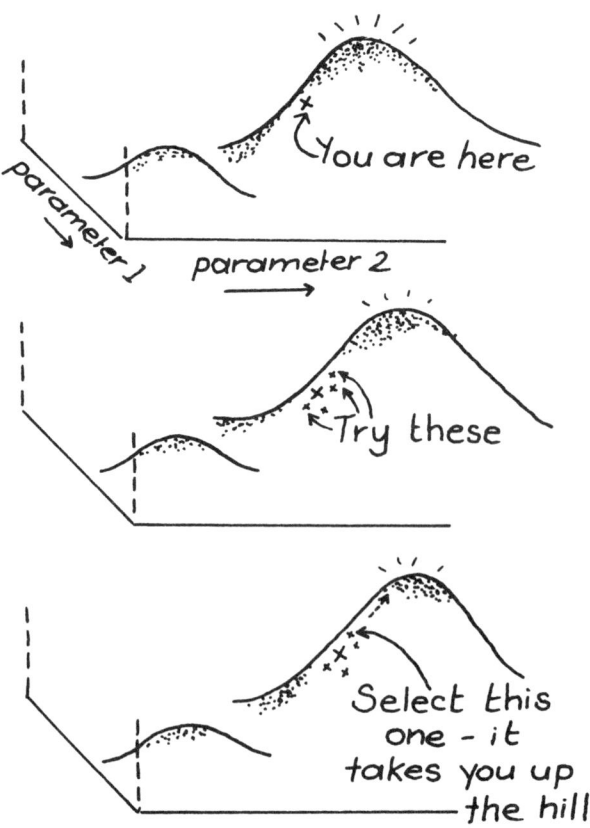

that it has just come up with, looks at all the solutions that it could get by juggling the various parameters of the problem, and picks the one that improves the match between its current solution and the optimal one. In practice this match is calculated by a *heuristic* that estimates how similar a solution is to the ideal. It is often quite easy to tell how far from a final solution a particular attempt is, although producing that attempt may be very hard. Thus the program climbs the hills on the 'solution' graph.

Hill climbing only finds a *locally* optimal solution. It will climb the nearest hill. If this is not the only hill on the graph, then it may not be the best solution. Genetic algorithms and simulated annealing approaches may get round this by statistical methods. Hill-climbing algorithms can only work if the function determining the 'height' is continous, i.e. the landscape does not contain any bottomless chasms.

There are a number of names for the 'height' of the hill, i.e. for the value determined by the heuristic which tells you how far from a solution you are: it can be called 'computational energy', 'objective function' or 'cost function' in different applications.

HOPFIELD NET

Neural nets

A Hopfield net is one of the first types of neural net. Hopfield nets differ from other neural nets as follows.

1. The neurones are capable of graded, analogue responses, not all-or-nothing responses.
2. Each neurone has an internal capacitance, which is the equivalent of a small internal memory of its last input, and a 'leakage current' which slowly dissipates this memory with time.
3. The neurones in the net do not have to fire at the same time (i.e. the net is asynchronous).

In addition, the connections between neurones are symmetrical, so that if neurone I stimulates the activity of neurone J, then neurone J will stimulate the activity of neurone I. This is not essential for the net to function, but was a basic assumption in Hopfield's analysis.

Each neurone sums its various inputs, and then produces an output dependent upon (but not equal to) the input for a given time, after which its response slowly declines.

Hopfield nets have been shown to be capable of solving some problems that are NP-hard (see *NP*) for conventional computers. One such is the *travelling salesman problem*, which the net can answer with a near-optimal path in only a few dozen steps while a conventional computer would take millions.

See also: Neural nets, Connectionism

HUMAN FACTORS RESEARCH

General
computer
term

Many of the tasks that AI will help people with in the future will require the computer to communicate much more intimately with the user than ever before. But what will the interfaces look like? How will they behave? What sort of dialogue will people want when they use a computer?

These important questions pin-point various areas of research which go under the name of 'human factors' or 'human-computer interaction (HCI)'.

See also: Cooperative system

HYPERCUBE

Hardware

Hypercube architecture is a way of connecting the processors in a parallel-processing system together. Mathematically a hypercube is a four-dimensional cube, but the concept here means that the processors are connected as if they were at the vertices of a four-, or many-dimensional cube. This architecture is a trade-off between the need for each processor to be able to communicate with every other processor, and for there to be neither too many paths between processors (leading to an impossibly large number of connections) nor too few (so that processors have to spend much of their time passing messages on to other processors).

Hypercube architecture was originally described in the 1940s by the writer Robert Heinlein in the story 'And he built a crooked house'.

See also: Parallel processing

HYPERMEDIA

General
computer
term

Hypermedia is the generic name given to a new style of information system which presents information on the screen not sequentially page by page, but in an animated, interactive form. Typically information in such a system can be imagined as a network of nodes containing text, graphics, application programs and so on. The ease with which hypermedia information can be accessed is a priority: more conventional information systems put the emphasis on the data the system contains.

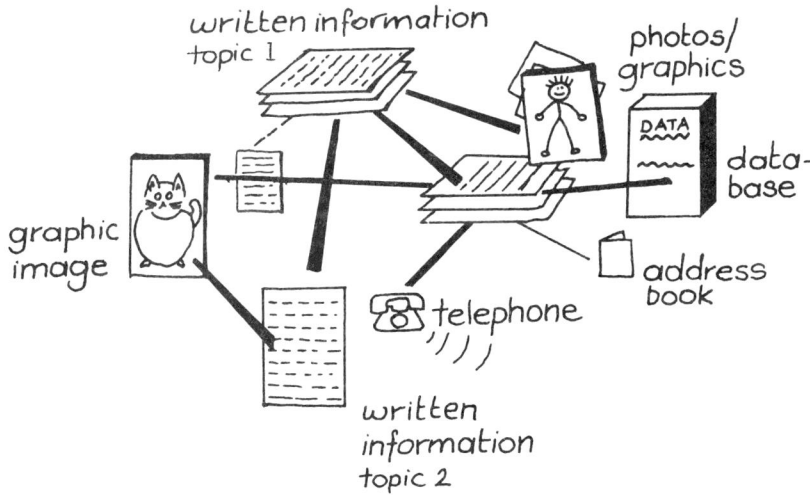

In 1988, the Apple computer company introduced the first free hypermedia package named HyperCard. Up until then, hypermedia systems had largely remained the province of academic institutions. The approach taken by Apple emphasizes the ability to construct high-quality graphics, an object-orientated programming model, and an easy-to-write programming language. This last feature allows people to write hypermedia applications without requiring a formal computer-science training.

In common with other hypermedia systems, HyperCard presents information to the user as a series of 'cards' arranged in a stack, a stack itself representing a node in the network of computer-held information.

As an example of a stack, take an imaginary computerized address book. Although really a simple database application, the address book looks fairly realistic on the screen: it has a spiral bound cover and letters down the side. By clicking with the mouse on the letter of your choice, the address book opens at the page – or card – you want. Furthermore, if you click on a small telephone symbol, the computer rings a selected number.

At the bottom of each page are icons which, when selected, act as links to pages. When you click on the icon, you can be taken one page backwards, forwards, or even jump out of the address book to a completely new application.

Behind the scenes, what happens is determined by a small piece of program called a *script*. The idea is that, by making scripts easy to write, even a non-programmer (with patience) can make the links much richer than those of more conventional systems.

Hypermedia technology is still at an immature stage in its development. The hypermedia systems of the future are likely to be closely linked with expert-system technology: in hypermedia systems today, it is generally the user who takes the initiative and decides what information he would like to see next. In the future, an expert system may intervene and question the user before displaying further information. Such 'mixed initiative' systems have many applications. For example, you might envisage on-screen catalogues which not only have pictures and text describing what is for sale, but will question you, where appropriate, to establish what product will precisely suit your needs.

See also: Human-factors research

INDUCTION

Logic

Induction is the form of logical inference which allows general conclusions to be drawn from particular examples. Although it is impossible to draw a logically rigorous conclusion using induction, its power to provide correct results most of the time is such that it is widely used in everyday life. Induction is how toddlers, and indeed the rest of us, learn things, but can lead the learner right up the garden path. Babies usually learn, from long exposure to nappies, woolly rabbits and mummy, that everything is soft. This leads to problems when they walk into furniture, cars and so on. Thus while induction is very useful, it must be used with great care.

Learning by induction goes in three stages:

1. *Induction* – making the first generalization, i.e. forming a hypothesis;
2. *Specialization* – discovery that the generalization was too wide, and only applies to a sub-class of the objects, i.e. narrowing hypotheses;
3. *Generalization* – discovery that the generalization is too narrow, and actually can cover more objects that you thought.

Some expert systems include learning systems which use induction to produce general rules from the specific data in them. Among the ways of doing this are *disjunct* and *conjunct manipulation*: adding OR makes a statement more general (Mary has red OR green hair), adding AND makes it more specific (Mary has red hair AND green shoes). This is quite simple to program in logic languages like Prolog: however, like our own induction, it can give rise to errors.

Induction can also mean the production of a current in a conductor by a varying magnetic field, the introduction of someone to a new social group or career, or a way of producing babies. None of these senses is widely used in AI!

See also: Deduction, Learning

INFERENCE ENGINE

Expert
systems

The term 'inference engine' is associated with expert systems. It is used to describe the part of the program which interprets the expert-system rules. When you ask an expert system a question, it is the inference engine that decides which facts and rules to use in determining the answer. The two most common methods used by inference engines to process rules are *forward chaining* and *backward chaining*. An example of each is given in its separate entry.

See also: Expert systems

INTERPRETER

General
computer
term

This is a computer program that interprets other computer programs, written in a high-level language like Basic or Lisp, into machine-code instructions which the computer can carry out. Thus the interpreter's overall function is to allow the computer to 'understand' a language like Basic by working on small elements of a program – usually single lines – and translating them as it goes.

Interpreters have a major advantage over compilers, and a major disadvantage. The advantage is that the computer runs the program as it is interpreted. Thus if line 17 contains an error, the interpreter will stop and allow you to correct it before going on to line 18.

The disadvantage is that the interpreter has to decode each line as it goes, even if it has decoded it 100 times before. The decoding stage is part of the running stage, and consequently running such a program is much slower.

Both interpreters and natural-language processing systems translate high-level language into lower-level equivalents. However, interpreters require a complete language specification to work, whereas NLP systems must be able to cope with the ambiguity of natural langauge.

See also: Compiler

INTUITION

Theory/
Philosophy

A criticism of AI is that, by proceeding solely through logic and mathematical methods, it cannot embrace the true mark of intelligence – intuition. Roger Penrose (in *The Emperor's New Mind*) has recently argued that the whole concept of an intelligent machine is flawed because no current method even considers the part that an intuitive leap of thought makes to intelligence.

Intuition in this context means two different things. Everyday intuition usually means little more than our expectations. We have an intuitive feel about how cars should behave, what the weather will do, or what someone is going to say next, but psychological studies have shown that this is almost entirely due to our having seen cars, weather and our friends behave in this way before. Thus a counter-intuitive event is simply an unexpected one. In this sense, computers could easily have intuition if they had a large enough memory of what went before.

In a more creative context, intuition is the leap from incomplete or inconsistent information to a unified explanation of it. It is not clear how much of this intuition is also due to extensive experience which could be formulated as production rules and how much is due to non-logical thought.

See also: Simulation v. emulation

KNOWLEDGE BASE

Expert
systems

The knowledge base is the part of an AI system that stores the facts, rules and concepts about a particular area of expertise. For example, the knowledge base of a system that diagnosed plant diseases would contain information about symptoms of illness in plants. During the course of a consultation, the inference engine would use the information contained in the knowledge base to come to conclusions.

As you might suspect, the knowledge in a knowledge base is highly structured in such a way that the inference engine can both access and use it. Common ways of representing knowledge are as follows.

1. You can present the knowledge as a series of facts and rules, either *procedural*, for example:

    do X if Y and Z happen
    to do X, first do Y

    or *declarative*, for example:

    X is true
    X is true if Y and Z are true
    All Y have the attribute Z
    X is a type of Z

2. You can group information about particular objects or ideas and represent this information as a *frame*. Each frame has a number of slots which may be filled with, for example, values of attributes (colour, size, age etc.), links to other frames, rules and instructions.
3. You can base the knowledge base on a semantic net of interrelated concepts.

An advantage of representing knowledge using rules, as opposed to 'conventional' programming techniques, is the maintainability of the knowledge base. A large system written in, say, Basic or Cobol, is very difficult to follow. The code may be hundreds of pages long and yet it is hard to say at any particular point in the program what is actually going on. Similarly questions about how the code handles a particular task ('How does the program deal with invoices to companies who have ordered in bulk?' or 'Does the program know about the discount we offer on our spotty pyjamas?') may be hard to answer particularly if the code is several years old and has been badly maintained.

By contrast, a program written as a set of rules may even be comprehensible to the non-programmer.

KNOWLEDGE ELICITATION

Expert
systems

Knowledge elicitation is the process of extracting expertise from human beings with a view to constructing an expert system. This is part of the process of knowledge engineering which is carried out by specialized computer analysts called *knowledge engineers*.

Successful knowledge elicitation involves both finding out what expertise the evisaged expert system should contain, and also discussing with the client how it might be used in the context of his organization. Neither of these tasks is easy: for a serious system, several months may elapse before knowledge engineers and client are clear about what the system will and will not do. During this time, the knowledge elicitor, who may have no knowledge at all about the domain in which he must work, must untangle a whole maze of expertise and formalize it into the sort of representations which form the basis of the eventual program.

In talking to the expert, the knowledge engineer must be something of a diplomat and detective. This is because human expertise is never that easy to extract.

For a start there is the incomprehensible nature of what the expert says. Experts invariably think they are speaking plainly and simply about their subject. They have gone to great pains to be sympathetic and, because you are a computer scientist, they use what to them are the simplest of terms and concepts. It seems incredible that you still cannot understand what they are saying. Accountants, for example, are amazed when even basic accounting terms are perceived as gibberish to other mortals. Surely even a computer scientist must know what a 'general ledger' is, have at least an inkling of 'journal voucher' and 'audit detail'? Not necessarily. So the knowledge engineer must play the part of the student and put up his hand and ask.

It's not just the terminology that confuses; it's how everything fits together. Finding out what is really important in a domain and what is actually a minor detail can be very challenging. A simple question will trigger an enthusiastic lecture on a topic you thought was unimportant. A question concerning what you thought was a major point may provoke a monosyllabic answer.

For the really tricky situation, there are various formal knowledge-elicitation techniques to resort to. For example, you can use cards upon which you write one or other concept or term. You randomize the cards and ask the expert to split them into two groups. Then you establish on what basis he grouped the cards. This enables you to establish more clearly how different concepts in his area are related.

Another method is to get one of the knowledge-engineering team to mimic the envisaged expert system. The 'expert system' communicates on paper with the user just as it would, once built, via the screen. This exercise gives a good idea of the accuracy of the envisaged expert system in handling queries and tests to see if the domain is adequately represented.

At the end of the day, what you want is an overview of the subject with a good understanding of the main concepts the eventual expert system will contain. There are various ways of putting your ideas up for discussion: entity relationship diagrams, decompositional diagrams, semantic nets and so on. These semi-formal methods can be used to discuss ideas critically: they provide a focus for discussion. Later, they can be turned into more formal representations of the domain.

See also: Knowledge engineering

KNOWLEDGE ENGINEERING

Expert
systems

Knowledge engineering is the process of extracting human expertise and then expressing it in expert-system form. Knowledge engineering therefore includes the process of *knowledge elicitation*, where the computer analyst (or knowledge engineer) interviews experts and researches the domain.

For a large expert system, a team of knowledge engineers may work for two years or more before completing their task. Such a team may contain a range of staff, from psychologists, concerned with the interface the final product will have (see *human-factors research*), to programmers who actually write the computer code. Between these two extremes the team may include analysts skilled in examining the client's needs closely, and also people skilled in interviewing, enthusiastic presentations and office politics.

To give some idea of what knowledge engineering entails, we have given a very simplified outline of the progress of a totally imaginary project to design an expert system. The system in question is to help salesmen to configure a complicated computer system for a large company. Following a consultation by a salesman, the expert system is to produce a diagram of the computer system that would suit the customer's needs, and help with the procedures associated with ordering the components.

Month 1 The knowledge engineers explain how an expert system might help the sales force to configure computer systems. The sales manager only vaguely understands, but agrees that the idea is certainly worth further study.

Month 2 Early stages of analysis. The knowledge engineers make numerous visits to speak to salesmen and managers about the project. Answers to the following questions are sought.

1. What is the expert system supposed to do? Where and how do we acquire knowledge about the domain?

2. What sort of hardware has the client got to run the expert system?
3. What sort of interface is the system to have? Should it be menu-driven or are the salesmen happy to communicate simply by yes/no answers? Does the system need to use graphics?
4. Does the system need to interface to spreadsheets, databases or other software?
5. What sort of output should the system have?
6. Who will be responsible for the system once it is installed? Who will maintain it? Will the rules be updated by a technical person or 'novice'?
7. Is the system likely to grow in size in the future?

Month 3   The knowledge engineers create a model of how they think the computer company currently processes the orders for the items it sells. This model includes information on discounts to particular customers, discounts on large volumes of sales and even takes into account exchange rates.

The team also draws up a taxonomy of computer parts, showing how the hundred-odd pieces of computer equipment it sells are interrelated. This representation will help to establish more clearly which cables are needed for which disk drive, what is the part number for the Spanish keyboard, and so on: essential knowledge when devising a computer system for a large customer.

Month 6   A prototype of the system is created. This reassures the client that things are on the right track. The scare that funding for the project may be cut at any moment recedes and everyone is happy.

Month 9   A more detailed specification for the expert system is created. This is then be converted into a better prototype. This prototype is reviewed by the client who suggests various changes in the interface and points out deficiencies in the system's knowledge. This process of design and review goes on for some time until ...

Month 20   The client is satisfied with the prototype. The specification now tallies with the client's requirements.

An engineering phase follows. During this, attention is given to the details of the user interface and maintenance facilities, the system's efficiency and the environment the system will run in. A phase of testing is also included before the eventual release of the product.

See also: Knowledge elicitation, Expert system

LEARNING

General AI
term

A wide range of techniques are used to allow computers to 'learn', i.e. to assimilate new information or procedures without a programmer writing a new program. Learning programs have to acquire information and then modify their behaviour appropriately. They are distinct from discovery programs, such as those designed to formulate new mathematical theorems, as learning programs have to acquire and assimilate external information, rather than explore the ramifications of their internal data.

Computer learning programs use a range of techniques at different levels, and often include elements of the following.

1. *Induction*, i.e. learning by generalization from specific examples.
2. *Candidate elimination*. This is a specific method of induction for a program learning the rules that govern something, such as a card game or the rules of the road in a foreign country. The program starts off with a large set of possible rules. It tests them, and weeds out ones which are too specific or too general. There are a range of approaches to this, including methods to select the most general or the most specific rule that is applicable, and test that one, and methods for generating new rules by making old ones more specific or more general.
3. *Genetic algorithms*. These use a random, additive search technique to find better and better versions of rules (or programs or other strings) by repeated 'mutation' and selection.
4. *Neural-net learning*. Neural nets do not have conventional algorithms, so methods that optimize algorithms are not applicable. However, they do require a learning algorithm, i.e. a method of training to modify the connections between neurons in the light of how well their output corresponds to what it ought to be. *Back propagation* is such a method.

Computer learning, a way of getting computers to modify their own programs, is a version of automatic programming. Progress on computer

117

learning has been poor. Computers' ability to learn from experience in any but very restricted, formal contexts (such as learning how to play card games) is unimpressive when compared to even very simple animals like flies or slugs. Indeed, it is from studying such simple animals that some of the background to neural-net approaches to learning developed, and with them the hope that neural nets would be substantially better at learning than more traditional, algorithmic approaches.

See also: Automatic programming

LEXICON

NLP

A lexicon is a computer-held dictionary. When you type a sentence into a computer which purports to understand ordinary human language, it is the lexicon which does the first stage and takes what you have typed and translates it into a form that the computer can further process.

For example, suppose you type in the word 'cat'. The computer looks up this word in the lexicon and sees that the particular sequence of letters maps onto a symbol PUSSY_CAT. PUSSY_CAT is then how the computer will from now on 'see' the word 'cat'. More than one word in the human language may map onto the same computer symbol so that the computer can accept a greater number of words. For example, 'cat', 'kittikins' and 'kittie' may, for simplicity, be translated as PUSSY_CAT.

There has been a tendency in recent years to enrich the lexicon to include more information about given words and the role they play in a sentence. Thus the lexicon may assume certain functions otherwise done by a grammar: the lexicon may, for example, have information about whether nouns are in the plural or the singular and whether verbs are in the past or the present. Such is the case in the simple lexicon shown below.

```
the   →   (the determiner)
kitty →   (pussy_cat noun sing)
cat   →   (pussy_cat noun sing)
dog   →   (dog noun sing)
mouse →   (mouse noun sing)
mat   →   (floor_covering noun sing)
sat   →   (verb sit (+ past))
on    →   (on prep)
```

See also: Parser, Natural-language processing

LIGHTHILL REPORT

Funding

In 1972 Sir James Lighthill chaired a committee set up by the UK's Science and Engineering Research Council to evaluate the research now known as artificial intelligence. His conclusions, that work on general-purpose problem-solving programs was dubious and should take second place to closely defined research on specific techniques, were interpreted outside the computing community as a blanket condemnation of AI. He considered that work on 'toy domains' was unlikely to be applicable to real-world problems because the latter were too complex, so the combinatorial explosion would render the solutions useless. Lighthill was particularly critical of some of the exaggerated claims in the area of robotics. British AI languished as a result of the report until the reflected glory of the Fifth Generation Projects initiative in Japan increased its political profile.

See also: Combinatorial explosion

LISP

Prog.
techniques

Lisp is a symbolic processing language which represents associations between objects, numbers and other symbols by using a structure called a list. Lisp is an acronym for List Processor.

The idea of processing symbols with lists was used as early as 1956 in a program called The Logic Theorist. This program was written in a language called IPL (Information Processing Language), a low-level language which was difficult to use. Lisp was evolved as an easier-to-use, high-level language based on IPL.

The hallmark of Lisp must be its brackets, an unmistakable feature of any program. These are used to delineate lists within lists (see *List processing*). Lists contain items of data which are processed by procedures or functions: Lisp is a functional programming language.

Since its early days, Lisp has undergone continued development. There are now dozens of Lisps on the market. Inevitably many of the dialects of Lisp are incompatible. One group of Lisps, known as the East Coast group, is largely incompatible with the West Coast group.

The East Coast dialects of Lisp are descended from a version of Lisp called MacLisp, created at the MIT AI lab (Mac supposedly stands for Machine-Aided Cognition and is nothing to do with the Macintosh computer). A kind of Lisp called Common Lisp has now been widely accepted as the standard Lisp within the East Coast community. Versions of Common Lisp are available for PCs. East Coast Lisps include Symbolics Lisp, Franz Lisp, C-Lisp and PSL.

West Coast Lisp actually originated in the Boston area, from a company called Bolt, Baranek and Newman. When a group of their computer scientists moved to Palo Alto in California, their development work on Lisp moved with them. Today, the best-known West Coast Lisp is InterLisp, which has grown into a powerful and flexible development tool.

Lisp is generally an interpreted language. This means that a Lisp *interpreter* translates each instruction into machine code as it is needed during the execution of a program. Contrast this to C, Pascal and Fortran which are usually compiled: the entire program needs to be compiled into a runnable form before it can be used.

See also: Interpreter, Compiler, Lisp chip, List processing

LISP CHIP (LISP MACHINE)

Hardware

Lisp chips and Lisp machines are pieces of hardware designed to run Lisp programs. Most computers' CPUs are designed to perform operations needed to run programs written in languages like Basic or Fortran, so they have single machine-code instructions for things like JUMP-IF-NUMBER-ZERO and SEARCH-FOR-NON-ZERO-NUMBER. This means that Fortran programs can be compiled into very efficient machine code for these computers, but Lisp cannot because it has a different structure. A Lisp machine has a different set of machine-code instructions, including single instructions for CRD and CAR, two standard Lisp procedures. Lisp machines are based around customized microchips called Lisp chips. Lisp machines can also have automated 'garbage collection' (removal of the discarded pieces of data, like unwanted segments of lists, from memory) and other features useful to Lisp programmers.

A feature of Lisp machines is that their memory is arranged to make storing lists easy. Instead of a linear array of items, Lisp-machine memories contain pairs of elements, the first of which contains the data and the second of which points to the next item in the list.

See also: Lisp

LIST PROCESSING

Prog.
techniques

A list is a data structure used in many AI languages, but notably in Lisp. A list divides the data it represents into components which can be accessed independently and which can be hierarchically structured.

A list consists of a number of symbols grouped together by brackets. These symbols are then processed by procedures. For example,

PRINT FIRST (yellow, red, green, blue)

could be used to print the first symbol in the list (yellow, red, green, blue).

Non-programmers may be surprised at how versatile this simple idea of lists and procedures can be. The rules in an expert system can be represented in list form, as can the rules of grammar (in *natural-language processing*). To demonstrate lists as they can be used in very elementary Lisp programming, we have taken a favourite AI problem, the *missionaries and cannibals puzzle*, and given some idea how lists can be used to represent the different stages in solving it. The missionaries and cannibals problem is outlined in the entry on *classic puzzles*.

Certain problems tackled using AI techniques can be represented as a number of intermediate situations or *states* (see *search*). Lists are one way of representing states. In the missionaries and cannibals problem, lists can be used to represent the people on each bank of the river. For example:

(MMMC BOAT) three missionaries, one cannibal, and the boat
(CC)   two cannibals
( )   an empty list: nobody on the bank

Lists are manipulated by *procedures*. A procedure can therefore be used to transform one state to another within a search tree. The items listed can be removed, added, swapped around and so on.

124

In the missionaries and cannibals problem, moving people between banks can be simulated by a procedure which takes a list like (MM BOAT) and then extracts certain items from it. The items extracted are then added to the items associated with the other bank.

The point of the missionaries and cannibals puzzle is that certain lethal combinations of missionaries and cannibals left together on a bank should be avoided: too many cannibals, and the missionaries get eaten. How can such lethal combinations be specified? This bit of program defines when missionaries are eaten:

```
(DEFUN MISSIONARIES_EATENQ ( )
  (OR (MEATENQ LEFTBANK)  (MEATENQ RIGHTBANK)))

(DEFUN MEATENQ(BANK)
  (AND (>(NUMBER OF 'C BANK)  (NUMBER OF 'M BANK))
       (<(NUMBER OF 'M BANK)0)))
```

Missionaries are eaten, according to the code above, when they are too few in number on either the right or left bank. 'Too few' is defined as a situation where the number of cannibals (C) is greater than the number of missionaries (M).

The entire program for the missionaries and cannibals problem is many pages long and is not included here. We hope that the examples given will at least give a flavour of how lists can be used to represent stages in solving the puzzle.

See also: Classic puzzles, Lisp

LOGIC PROGRAMMING

Logic

Logic programming is a method whereby knowledge is represented and used according to certain laws of mathematical logic.

Logic programming originally grew out of research into automated inference. Inference is the process for which detectives are famous: from known facts and observations, conclusions are cleverly drawn. The method of inference that interested early researchers in logic programming was *resolution inference*. This type of inference is used to draw conclusions expressed in a formal language called *predicate calculus*.

A very simple example of predicate calculus is as follows.

Facts: Nibbles is a rabbit
        All rabbits adore lettuce
So: Nibbles adores lettuce

Of course, the overall concepts handled by a logic program are much more complicated than this, but the elements of a logic program, the individual expressions of which it is composed, are of this level of simplicity.

Apart from simple statements of fact (like those above), rules of the form

A is the case if conditions B, C, D, E ...

are also allowed. Rules of this type allow the programmer to express the logical relationship between objects and ideas, albeit in an extremely concise and rigid way. It requires great skill and ingenuity to transform everyday ideas into the logical statements that a logic program will allow.

You can get some idea of the kind of thinking required of a logic programmer by trying to state logically and in a foolproof way how to join two lists of words together. When is it generally true that a list of words starting

127

XYZ is joined on to a second list of words ABC to give the new structure XYZABC?

One possibility is to generalize about the order of the items first when the lists are separate, and then again when the lists are joined together. Any logical relationships between unjoined and joined lists can then be made explicit as a set of rules.

Lists may thought of as having a head element H, with tail elements T. You can write a list in a kind of shorthand: in Prolog, a common logic programming language, [H|T] means a list with head element H and tail T.

Suppose you start with the list [H|T] and join on to it a second list, called L. A new list with a longer tail results. However, this new list still has the head element H. The new and longer tail is conventionally denoted by R. In Prolog we can state:

append ([H|T, L, [H|R])   appending [H|T] gives [H|R]
append (T, L, R).   appending T to L gives R

On the other hand, if you have a list containing no items at all (denoted [ ] meaning an empty list) then gluing this onto list L leaves list L unchanged:

append ([ ], L, L)   appending [ ] to L gives L

These relationships are illustrated in the diagram opposite. On their basis, the complete append predicate is written as follows:

append   ([ ], L, L)
append   ([H|T], L, [H|R]) if append (T, L, R)

These two lines are a logic program for the append predicate. They define completely and exhaustively what is logically involved in joining two lists together.

One thing you may notice is that the append predicate is recursive. In other words, the definition of 'append' called upon append itself, the very relation you are defining. The use of recursion features strongly in Prolog.

See also: Prolog

MACHINE TRANSLATION

General AI
term

Computer translation means the use of a computer to perform part of the task of translating text from one 'source' language to another 'object' language. All the commercial systems that do this, however, need a human to convert the program's output into idiomatic language.

The earliest translation systems worked as follows. First they performed simple grammatical analysis on the original text, then they looked up the words and phrases in a dictionary to give corresponding words and phrases in the target language. Where there was ambiguity, choices were made according to the word's context, but in a very simple way.

By the late 1960s these simple methods were found wanting, and research therefore switched to more indirect methods of translation, where there was more emphasis on context and semantics. This coincided with Chomsky's work on transformational grammar, applied here by attempting to get the program to translate a sentence into a standard representation. However, the ambiguity and uncertainty of language remained a problem and results were not very good.

Today interest in machine translation has arisen in Europe, particularly in connection with the EEC countries. Two projects, SYSTRAN and EUROTRA have been funded. An example of a SYSTRAN translation is given below. Note that the main mistake the computer makes (it thinks we are talking about people of different nationalities when in fact we are talking about languages of different nationalities) is through complete lack of understanding of what the text actually means.

French   L'utilisation de FSSRS est basée sur un système de menus hierarchisés d'un usage assez aisé. L'utilisateur a la possibilité de travailler en Français, Anglais ou Allemand. Ce manuel de consultation et le manuel 'Contenu de la base' ne sont disponibles qu'en Français et en Anglais; cependant si la demande existe ils pourraient être traduits en Allemand.

English translation, by machine The use of FSSRS is based on a system of hierarchized fragments rather easy use. The user has the possibility of working as Frenchman, Englishman or German. This consultation handbook and the handbook 'Contents of the base' is available only as Frenchmen and as Englishmen; meanwhile if the request exists they could be translated into a German.

EUROTRA envisages an intermediate European 'representation' into which all source texts could initially be transformed, and from which the translation into any of the object languages would be made. This is a daunting objective, and progress has been slow.

See also: ESPRIT, Natural-language processing

META KNOWLEDGE

Theory/
Philosophy

Meta-knowledge is knowledge about knowledge. This is distinct from object knowledge, which is knowledge about what is possible: how things behave and the characteristics they have.

In expert systems, which contain perhaps hundreds of rules, *meta-rules* tell the system which rules to apply, and in what order. In other words, the meta-knowledge enables the system to use the facts it contains. Some examples of meta-rules are given in the entry of that name.

Meta-language. A language is a set of codes which describe the world, or part of it. A meta-language is therefore a set of codes that describes a

language. More narrowly and less philosophically, a meta-language is an intermediate between the language which is the start of a translation process and the target language.

Meta-plan. A program involved in planning may use an intermediate state between the plan and the facts on which it is based. This is sometimes called a meta-plan: a plan of how to plan. Meta-plans, and indeed meta-knowledge, can occur at several levels, starting with a strategic level, with more detailed tactical levels below the strategic one.

Other 'meta'-terms used in computing are meta-assembler (a program which will generate an assembler program from a description of a computer's machine code language) and meta-interpreter.

See also: Object knowledge

META RULE

Expert
systems

A meta-rule in an expert system controls the firing of other, more factual rules (see *Meta-knowledge*). For example, an expert system about skin rashes might contain the following factual rules.

1. If spots itchy and many spots visible then suggest bed bug bites.
2. If small spots and forming blisters then suggest chicken-pox.
3. If spots localized and small numbers then suggest mosquito bites.

These in turn might be applied according to the following meta-rules.

1. If small child then rules 1 and 3 particularly apply.
2. If been camping then try rule 1 first.
3. If older person then rules 1 and 3 unlikely to apply.

MINIMAX TECHNIQUE

Games and
toy domains

The minimax technique is a procedure for assigning values to the nodes of a game tree, to improve the efficiency of search.

Suppose we invent a game for which you score as follows:

+1 for winning the game
−1 for losing the game
 0 for drawing the game

This situation is represented by the diagram below. The game tree shows the last three moves left in the game involving a player and his opponent. It is the player's turn to move. The terminal nodes of the tree are marked with their values to the player. The minimax technique allows the computer to calculate, from the values of the terminal nodes, the values of the rest of the nodes in the tree.

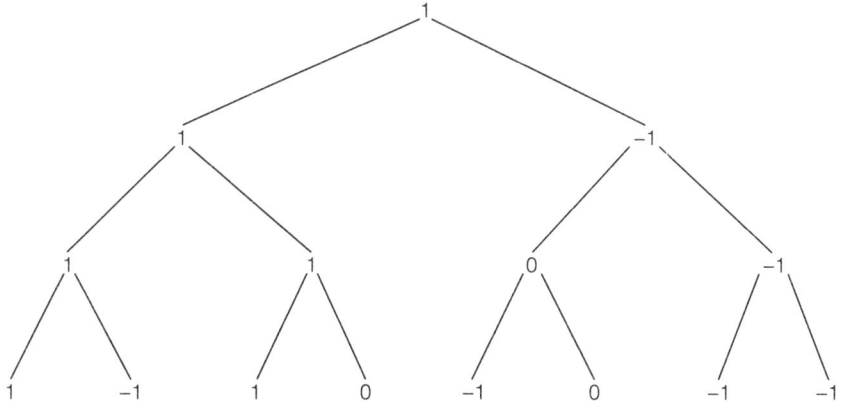

The rules for assigning values are as follows:

1. If it is the player's turn to move (the node is an OR node: see *AND–OR tree*) then the value of that node is the maximum value of its children.

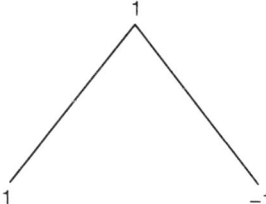

2. If it is the opponent's turn to move (the node is an AND node), then the value of that node is the minimum value of its children.

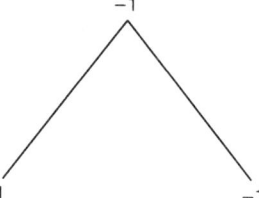

Once values have been assigned to nodes, these can be used to find the path the player shoud use to win the game. To win, the player should move through nodes of the highest value. Meanwhile, his opponent should move through nodes of the lowest value. A node of low value is a bad move from the player's point of view, and consequently a good move for the opponent.

It is conventional to call the player MAX and his opponent MIN. The minimax technique forms the basis of the more elaborate technique of alpha-beta pruning. This is used to limit the number of nodes investigated where the search tree is very large, as in chess.

See also: Search, Alpha-beta pruning

MODEL BASED VISION

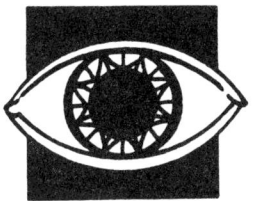

Vision

This is a vision approach which starts with a list of possible things that the camera might be looking at, and then checks to see if corresponding features actually occur in the picture which the computer is analysing. This contrasts with the 'bottom-up' approach of finding out what picture features there are, what real-world surfaces could be causing those features, and hence what objects might have those surfaces. The latter approach could find anything, in principle, in a picture. However, it is very hard to do. The former approach can only find what it is looking for, but can find it much more quickly.

The classical model-based (or model-driven) vision system was described in 1965. In it a simple edge-detection system draws a line drawing of the view (of *blocks world*), and then looks for clues about what it is looking at. For example, three lines joining in a figure Y are a good clue that this is the nearest corner of a cube or brick. The program then goes back to the image and looks for more clues for the existence of a cube. As for all blocks-world applications, this is hard to generalize to the wider world.

MONOTONIC REASONING

Theory/
Philosophy

In logic programming, you present the computer with a number of facts and then allow the computer to work logically through them, resolving any conclusions that follow: in a sense, logic programming relies on a 'logician in a computer'. If the reasoning employed by this 'logician' were to use logic of an unadulterated form, the system would be monotonic. In logic programming, the reasoning employed departs from straightforward logic in the classical sense and is in some respects 'impure'. The reasoning used in logic programming systems is therefore non-monotonic.

The exact differences between monotonic and non-monotonic reasoning are, to all but the logician, rather subtle. In monotonic reasoning, every new fact added to those facts already present, must in no way cause inconsistencies in the system. When you add a new fact to the database of facts already known, it may be necessary to remove logically conflicting pieces of information. Everything that was logically provable before must remain provable after the new fact has been added.

With non-monotonic reasoning, conflicts are allowed between facts in the database. Where a large number of facts are in use, non-monotonic reasoning makes more sense. For this reason, computer systems generally use non-monotonic reasoning, forsaking certain aspects of pure mathematical logic in the process.

The favourite demonstration of the problems of monotonic reasoning involves birds and flightless birds, and the logical connection between them. The flightless bird is invariably called Tweety and in many research papers Tweety is a penguin (a friend of Tweety is Nikita).

Suppose you have the following database on which you wish to base a logical argument:

X can fly if X is a bird;
X is flightless if and only if X cannot fly;
Tweety is a bird.

If you now add

Tweety is flightless,

then, using logic in unadulterated form, the database becomes inconsistent. This happens because it is possible to derive that, Tweety being a bird:

Tweety can fly.

With non-monotonic reasoning, the fact that Tweety is flightless poses no problems.

See also: Closed-world assumption, Logic programming

NAIVE PHYSICS

Theory/
Philosophy

This means physics without many numbers. For example, naïve physics
might have a rule that if you throw something, it will fall to the ground
some distance away, and the harder you throw it, the further it will go.
Things thrown up eventually come down: the harder they are thrown up, the
longer they take to come back again. None of this is quantitative, and if

there are any comparisons between different 'experiments', they rely on such concepts as 'bigger' or 'further' rather than '1.72 times'. Relatively simple number systems, such as '0, 1, 2, many', or 'less than 5' v. 'more than 5', are also often thought of as embodying a 'naïve physics' approach. This contrasts with 'real physics', with its emphasis on accurate enumeration.

Humans use naïve physics to reason about the real world. Knowledge-based systems can use naïve physics rather than trying to model the world exactly in numerical terms. This is a version of *compiled knowledge*, and so is easier to use, but is liable to break down in exceptional cases, where the assumptions of the original calculations or models have changed.

See also: Natural-language processing

NANOTECHNOLOGY

Hardware

Whereas the conventional machine consists of gears, pistons, pumps and so on, the nanomachine is constructed of molecular components. With an eye to the future, K. Eric Drexler speculates in his book *Engines of Creation, the Coming Era of Nanotechnology* that machinery of the order of a millionth of a millimetre in size (one nanometre is 10^{-9} metre) will lead to advances in AI, advances in manufacturing design, and even to developments in medicine and space technology.

During the 1970s and 1980s biochemists discovered a number of themes used by all living organisms at the molecular level. They discovered, for example, that some molecules were 'catchers', others 'transporters'. There were also 'replicators', 'repairers', 'converters', 'fuelling agents' and many others.

Drexler, realizing that each molecule must be tightly engineerined by evolution to carry out its designated task, takes things a step further and suggests that human engineers might actually employ these clever machine components (or at least derivations of them) for their own devices.

Drexler envisages that assembler and replicator molecules, for instance, could be used to manufacture a rocket engine. He suggests that a rocket engine could be 'grown' inside a steel vat 1–2 m tall filled with thousands of nanomachines receiving instructions from a tiny nanocomputer. In the same way that fermentation chambers are filled with a nutrient broth to promote growth of yeasts, so the vat would be filled with aluminium and oxygen-rich compounds, fuel and other chemicals needed by the nanomachines as they manufactured the engine parts.

Assemblers would position themselves correctly in the vat and then extrude a form of aluminium oxide or a kind of interlocking carbon with the necessary strength and heat resistance for a rocket engine. Drexler also imagines that the assemblers would posess flagella to keep the current of nutrients flowing past them steady, rather like the cells of marine sponges under water.

Once the rocket engine had been made, it would be washed down and then removed from the vat. It would appear, according to Drexler, 'seamless' and 'gem-like'.

Drexler suggests many other uses of nanotechnology. The tiny nanomachines might be useful as repairers of human tissue, for example. A number of nanomachines could enter the body and locate and remove diseased material.

In the case of AI, Drexler points out that programming AI will require new science: current technology does not make true AI possible. Nanotechnologists, he says, may use virus-sized molecular machines to study the functions of the brain, cell by cell. This, he thinks, may give true insight into the workings of the brain and lead to many advances in AI itself: after learning how neurones work, engineers will build analogous devices based on advanced nanoelectronics and nanomachines.

Although nanotechnology is still a speculative science, the idea of using lifelike qualities of organic molecules is growing in popularity. Recently, Julius Rebek Jr at MIT announced the creation of a compound called osine triacid ester which has a life like ability to reproduce itself. The compound grabs two simple molecules, holds them in a position in which they automatically join together, and then releases the new molecule, a duplicate of itself.

NATURAL KIND

Theory/
Philosophy

This is a term used in discussions of knowledge and knowledge-based systems. Natural kind is a general name for any group of things which fall 'naturally' into a class or group. Thus 'dog' is a 'natural' sort of group: we all clearly recognize what is and is not a dog. Other categories, like 'intelligence' and 'microcomputer', have no such universally agreed, real-world counterpart.

Ideally, the knowledge bases of expert systems should be structured to represent natural kinds, so that access of the data held on 'Cerberus' automatically conjures up all the various attributes of doggishness such as teeth, hair, and barking at passing cars, but not irrelevant information, like the fact that 'cauliflower' starts with the same letter. *Object-oriented programming* techniques try to do this. The only problem is that it is unclear whether natural kinds actually exist. Why is a wolf not a dog when a pink soft toy called 'Spot' is a dog? Why was ENIAC a computer when a modern pocket calculator, which has more memory and more processing power, is not?

The philosopher Wittgenstein had a lot to say on these and related problems, much of it apparently contradictory, and modern philosophers and sociologists contribute vociferously to this area. It is a good term to drop into conversation with computer scientists, but otherwise steer clear!

See also: Explicit v. tacit knowledge

NATURAL LANGUAGE INTERFACE

NLP

A natural-language interface is a program which allows you to communicate with a computer in human language. Also called natural-language front ends, such interfaces today only accept a limited form of language as input. The primary use of natural-language interfaces is in information retrieval from large databases. Databases are conveniently narrow and well-defined domains, so, although they may list thousands of facts, the range of questions a person is likely to ask about them remains relatively small. But people, even specialists, may phrase their questions in many different ways. How can a natural-language interface cope with this variety?

A number of different techniques are in use. Perhaps the easiest to understand are those used by LIFER, designed by Gary Hendrix of the Stanford Research Institute in 1977. LIFER uses a kind of grammar which, instead of looking for verbs, adjectives or other 'parts of speech' (see *Grammar*), sees sentences in terms of units of meaning.

Imagine an interface to a database containing stock information on paint stored in a large warehouse. This might use 'paint colour', 'paint type', 'coverage' and 'price' as basic units of meaning. An interface to such a database, if based on LIFER, might employ three programming tricks:

1. templates;
2. paraphrasing;
3. ellipsis.

A *template* is a standard form of sentence on to which other non-standard forms can be mapped. For example, the sentences

What is the price of lilac emulsion paint?
What is the coverage of red gloss paint?

both map onto the template:

(WHAT IS) ATTRIBUTE (OF) PAINT

Paraphrasing allows a particular phrase to mean the same thing as something else. For example:

LET: How many tins of yellow paint have you got?
MEAN: What is the volume of yellow paint in stock?

Ellipsis deals with queries which are not complete sentences. The meaning of such queries is based on the preceding query:

What is the coverage of yellow gloss paint?
Its price?
Its availability?

LIFER can also cope with incorrect spelling, and can interpret pronouns and synonyms.

LIFER is a relatively simple interface. It therefore has limitations as follows:

1. Conversation is strictly about a very limited domain.
2. The system cannot deal with disjunction (A OR B), quantification, implication or causality.
3. There are rigid restrictions on the kinds of data and the allowed relationships between items.

LIFER is over a decade old, and natural-language interfaces have progressed a lot since then, although many of the ideas mentioned are still in use. A very different approach to a natural-language interface is provided by the augmented transition network, or ATN.

Even if the grammatical constructs of a sentence are known, extracting meaning is quite another matter. Although some interfaces use parsing techniques coupled with some system to represent the meaning in sentences encountered, they are fallible and only operate within a strictly defined domain.

See also: Front end, Natural-language processing

NATURAL LANGUAGE PROCESSING

NLP

Natural-language processing (NLP) is a research area of artificial intelligence which aims to develop the means to interact with computers in natural (as opposed to computer) language. The interaction may be typed or spoken.

Since language, as we use it, is an expression of our own intelligence, it is hardly surprising that getting computers to understand what we say amounts to making computers fully intelligent too. AI researchers, in trying to address the issue of natural-language processing, have to contend with this fact, and realize that true natural-language communication with computers will probably not happen in their lifetime.

Meanwhile, NLP remains an exciting area of research, being at the intersection of linguistics, philosophy, psychology and computer science.

For a computer to interpret natural language, it needs the following types of knowledge:

1. knowledge about the acceptable sequence of words in a sentence (a knowledge of *grammar*);
2. knowledge of how people use words to express ideas and concepts;
3. knowledge of the laws of conversation, including a model of the personality, attitudes and level of understanding of the person being spoken to;
4. common-sense knowledge about the world.

The problem of grammar has already been tackled quite thoroughly. A number of grammars have been programmed which specify how words may be combined to form sentences. By using a 'syntactic' *parser*, a computer can split a sentence up into its parts of speech: verbs, nouns, adjectives and a representation of the sentence constructed. Once a program can split a sentence, it is fairly easy to assemble pieces of sentence together to generate answers in a grammatically correct format. Although most people would agree that the syntax of a sentence is important, many argue that this

147

information should be integrated with semantic knowledge. In other words, they believe that the meaning behind the sentence should be represented along with its 'surface' arrangement.

Knowledge of how people use words to express ideas and concepts is much harder to represent in a computer than the order and type of words in sentences. We are very ambiguous about what we mean and rarely spell out everything in black and white. Psychologists have suggested that when we hear a sentence spoken, we probably scan for many interpretations in parallel. For example, we take into account fashionable or cultural uses of certain words. We also apply general knowledge about the world, something that computers certainly do not have. Even in everyday conversation, we say things that people find easy to understand, but which the most advanced computer would not.

Suppose we describe an employee to a computer. Included in the description is the following:

He's the sort of person your mother would love: terribly good at sitting in a comfy chair watching the box.

A computer might register two positive attributes:

1. that your mother would approve of him;
2. that he has achieved excellence in a particular activity.

This is exactly the opposite of what we actually meant. Other sentences are simply ambiguous:

We saw Wembley stadium flying into London airport.

Only because of our general knowledge about the world do we know that it cannot be Wembley stadium that is flying.

Many methods have been developed for dealing with the meaning behind sentences in a very limited way. Case grammars, for example, render sentences into frame-like representations showing the function of different groups of words (who did what, what they did, etc.).

For a really natural conversation, you need to know something about the person you are talking to. Already some systems take into account whether you are a novice or an expert when they explain something to you, but they do so very crudely (see *Explanation systems* and *Cooperative systems*). The computer systems of the future may well speak to users in a polite and helpful way and possess infinite patience! Working systems of this type are, of course, a long way off.

A common-sense knowledge of the world is something all people have:

Objects fall down if nothing holds them up.
You catch a train by going to a station.

Computers have to be explicitly told (or be able to learn) such things. To avoid the problem of common-sense knoweldge, many systems of the future will still only operate within a very small and clearly defined domain.

NEATS AND SCRUFFS

General AI
term

Neats and scruffs represent two extremes of thought in AI research. The neats believe that logical and mathematical theories of thinking exist: that intelligence can be captured in some kind of formal theory.

The scruffs believe that in the knowledge lies the power: it is not any underlying theory of mathematics, but your knowing about something that allows you to solve the problem.

A scruff is interested in looking for practical ways of solving problems and is less concerned with the underlying theory.

NEGATION BY FAILURE

Prog.
techniques

Logic-programming languages such as Prolog are based on only a subset of logic (the horn clause subset of predicate calculus), and procedures are not provided for stating that things are true or false. Negation by failure is used as the next best thing.

Negation by failure is the assumption that something is false until it can be proved true.

Consider the fact that:

X likes strawberries if X does not live in Bristol.

You look in your address book. There is no mention of where John lives at all. So, if there is no proof that John lives in Bristol, this means that:

John does not live in Bristol

and it follows that John likes strawberries. In negation by failure, the evaluation of the condition 'not C' becomes the evaluation of the condition 'is C the case?'. So long as C cannot be proved to be the case, then 'not C' is taken to be TRUE.

Negation by failure rests on the notion that the logical axioms of the argument completely describe the domain. This is the essence of the *closed-world assumption*.

See also: Logic programing

NEURAL NETS

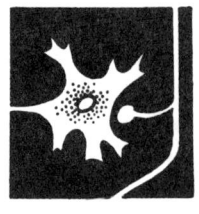

Neural nets

Neural nets are theoretical and research designs of computer which use simple processing units connected in parallel-processing arrays. The elements are modelled after nerve cells (neurones), and indeed are often called neurones. Neural nets fall into three types:

1. *biological models*: models of what goes on in nerve cells, both as individual cells and as small groups;
2. *cognitive models*: cognitive-science models of how we think;
3. *connectionist models*; model systems for computation, based on nerves and their behaviour.

AI is concerned primarily with the third type.

Single-layer nets are the simplest, but are of limited use. In two-layer nets the neurones are interconnected by 'axons': one layer receives input, the other generates output. The perceptron is the best-known of these models. Perceptrons can recognize shapes, a feat few conventional computers can manage. However, they cannot solve problems like computing 'exclusive OR'. For that a third layer of neurones in between the input and output layer is needed: this is called a 'hidden layer' and the neurones in it are sometimes called 'interneurones'.

152

Most neural-net studies are carried out in simulations, either on parallel computers of a more traditional type, particularly on transputers, or on normal (serial) machines. This last option is very slow, so when someone says that a neural-net model solves some particular problem very fast, he means that it is fast in terms of the number of cycles or time steps the whole net performs. This might take a long time in simulation.

The processor – neurones – in a neural net typically have a number of input lines (sometimes called dendrites, by analogy with real neurones), and one output line (sometimes called an axon), although the axon can branch to contact several dendrites. The contacts between axon and dedrite can be excitatory (i.e. they enhance the activity of the receiving neurone) or inhibitory. They produce graded signal responses, so a neurone performs a summing function on its inputs, and outputs a quantitative response.

There are three sorts of neurone used in the more generally studied connectionist nets, as follows.

1. *McCulloch-Pitts neurone.* This sort of element treats a neurone as a logical device: an AND or OR gate with numerous inputs and one output.
2. *Adaptive neurone.* This is a more complex element which sums inputs to produce a linear response. Adaptive neurones could be the basis of pattern-recognition circuits.
3. *Hopfield-net neurone.* This is the element used in Hopfield nets. It has a sigmoidal response to input stimulus, meaning that the output only increases by a given amount given an increase in input, after which it levels off; and no amount of extra input will make it increase further.

Neural nets are of interest to AI for two reasons. First, they are massively parallel computers, and hence offer advantages of speed in computation-intensive tasks; second, they offer a different approach to computing than the serial-processing, rule-based algorithmic approach of traditional AI. This has substantial potential for solving some intractable problems, such as pattern recognition in vision. In particular, neural nets 'learn' to solve problems in a fashion that is dependent on their structure and not on an externally input program.

Neural nets have had most success in solving two types of problems: highly connected problems and classification problems. Connected problems are ones in which the solution to one part of the problem is intimately connected to the solution to the other parts. The *task assignment* and *travelling salesman* problems are of this sort.

Classification problems are problems in which you have to decide in which of several classes an individual belongs. A neural net is 'trained' with examples of each of the classes, and is then shown a trial sample to classify into one of the classes. Neural nets have been used to classify faces (the WIZARD machine does this in 'real time', using specialist electronics to identify 'familiar' faces), census data and assembly line components.

See also: Connectionism, Task assignment problem, Travelling salesman problem

NP

General
computer
term

NP stands for non-deterministic polynomial, which describes a type of problem (or, more exactly, a type of solution). NP problems are very difficult when they are large.

The 'polynomial' term refers to our calculation of the amount of time it is going to take us to solve the problem. For example, suppose the problem is to find the largest number in a list. The amount of time taken to do this is proportional to the length of the list. Sorting the list into descending order by removing successive largest values takes a length of time proportional to the square of the length of the list. These are P problems: problems for which a solution can be found in a length of time described by a polynomial.

What about problems that are not P? The most dramatic type is the exponential problem: this is a problem for which the solution requires time determined by an exponential function of the size of the problem. An exponential function will always grow faster than a polynomial one eventually, so exponential problems always take more time than polynomial ones when they are large enough. One class of exponential problems comprises those search problems that suffer from the combinatorial explosion.

A 'halfway house' is the NP problem. This is not solvable in polynomial time. However, once you have a possible solution, you can check that it is correct in polynomial time. An example is sorting a list of numbers into ascending order. The time needed to sort the list increases exponentially as the size of the list increases. However, you can test whether a list is in order simply by looking at each item once, and confirming that it is larger than the one before it.

Whether a problem is P or NP depends on the algorithm chosen to solve it. Thus some NP problems can actually be P problems if we choose the right algorithm to solve them. A problem that is NP regardless of the algorithm chosen to solve it is called *NP-complete*. The *travelling salesman problem* is NP-complete. A related term, *NP-hard*, refers to the very rapid

155

increase in the time taken as the size of a problem increases: the travelling salesman problem is also NP-hard.

NP problems are not necessarily difficult to solve. They only take extreme lengths of time for very large problems: for a small version of the problem, the solution can be very fast. And there may be an approximate or heuristic solution which is also very fast: AI's role is often to find these approximate solutions.

See also: Algorithm, Combinatorial explosion

OBJECT KNOWLEDGE

General
computer
term

Object knowledge is knowledge about the legal (permissible) ways that symbols, ideas and objects can behave. This is in contrast to *meta-knowledge*, which consists of strategies for using the object knowledge you have. Whereas object knowledge is what you know, meta-knowledge is knowledge about what you know.

Take the following problem:

How do you produce the number 8 from the number 12, by adding or subtracting the number 2?

The object knowledge consists of the arithmetical moves you are allowed to make:

How to add 2
How to subtract 2

The meta-knowledge tells you how to use this knowledge to come to an answer:

Adding 2 to a positive number increases its size
Subtracting 2 from a positive number decreases it size
8 is a positive number
The size of 12 is greater than the size of 8
To produce a number greater than another number, increase its size
And so on...

OBJECT ORIENTED PROGRAMMING

Originally implemented by Xerox in the language SmallTalk, object-oriented programming has become increasingly popular in recent years as a method of structuring and representing information. It is used in many applications which draw on AI ideas and techniques.

Unless you are a programmer, object-oriented programming will always remain a bit mysterious; nevertheless we have attempted to give a brief explanation of what it involves.

One of the problems facing the programmer is how to set out data, and the procedures which act on such data, in an organized manner. Many of the earlier programming languages (such as Fortran) suffered from a problem called 'spaghetti code'. Programs written in these languages had so many 'go to' statements to tell the computer which parts of the program to branch to, that the code as a whole became impossible to understand, and hence to modify.

To avoid this problem, limited control structures such as

If ... then ... else ...
Do ... until ...
While X ... do the following ...

were introduced into programming languages to make it easier to see what was going on. Pascal and Algol 68 are examples of languages using this 'structured programming' approach popular in the 1970s.

Object-oriented programming offers a new approach. In it, the central theme is the 'object', a fragment of computer code encompassing everything to do with an idea or item the program uses. You might, for example, create an object 'employee' in a program for use by a personnel department. This object would carry attributes associated with it, such as address and job title. It is a simple matter to creat new 'instances' of the generic object (for

158

example, individual employees), and these offspring may inherit their parental attributes.

New 'classes' of employee can also be created: for example, those who work in the computer department.

An object not only consists of data; it also consists of 'methods'. A method gives an object the inherent ability to respond to 'messages'– communications from the user or from other objects. For example, a message may be used to change the job title of an employee or his address. Another message may cause a particular object to display, to the user, the values of certain attributes.

To give some idea of the object-oriented approach, here is a small (simplified) part of an imaginary program.

Define an employee object as a kind of person object.

Each employee object has:

a name, by default Joe Bloggs;
a job title, by default Engineer;
a salary, by default £10,000;
an employee grade, by default 0.

If I'm an employee object and I receive a message asking for my holiday entitlement, I query my employee grade and see if it's greater than 5.

If so, I reply '20 days', otherwise I reply '18 days'.

Note the following points.

1. The object known as 'employee object' has a number of attributes.
2. The 'employee object' may inherit attributes from a more generalized 'person object'.
3. The 'employee object' has the capacity to respond to messages asking for information about its attributes.
4. There are various rules to apply in response to messages.

Two kinds of messaging are used in object-oriented programs. In *synchronous messaging* the message is sent out and the program then waits patiently for a reply. This matches the procedural call of conventional programming languages where the program initiates a procedure and only resumes execution when the procedure has done whatever it should. *Asynchronous messaging* is rather like sending a letter through the post.

You send the message to its destination and then expect a reply to be posted back some time later. This style of messaging is used in distributed processing systems (networks) where immediate processing of messages is often not practical.

There are many object-oriented programming languages in existence, including Objective C, C++ and SmallTalk.

OPERATOR

General
computer
term

The word 'operator' turns up in a number of areas of AI carrying a mathematical meaning. An operator describes how to change data into processed data, i.e. how to perform an operation on the data. The '+' operator, meaning 'add these two numbers together', is an example. The 'in' or '$\in$' operator ('is an element of') tests whether one item is in a list or set of items. For example:

'dog *in* {cat dog mouse}' is *true*.

The spatial operator (in vision systems) is a function that can be applied to a digitized picture for edge detection. Operators are found in many areas of mathematics and programming, not just AI.

OPTICAL FLOW

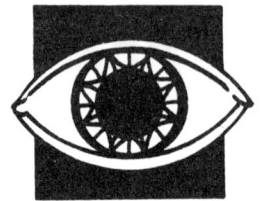

Vision

Optical flow is a way of representing how a picture moves. Usually, descriptions of computer-vision systems assume that the picture is going to stay still for the duration of the processing. However, information about the objects in the picture, as well as their motion, can be gleaned from how the picture changes. The motion is assumed to be continuous, and each point on the picture is said to flow from one place to the next. This is often visualized as a series of bars across the picture, the direction of the bar showing the direction that points in its vicinity are travelling and the length showing the speed.

PARADIGM

Theory/
Philosophy

A paradigm is a pattern used in interpreting the world and, by extension, a collection of ways of looking at and explaining the world. The term was popularized in scientific circles by Thomas Kuhn, who wanted to explain why different generations of scientists could explain exactly the same world with the aid of drastically different theories. (Kuhn said that they actually inhabit different worlds, but it is difficult to see how they went to the same restaurants if this is so.) 'Paradigm' has two meanings, one 'broad', one 'narrow'.

It can mean a whole set of theories and experimental demonstrations which support each other and which provide a coherent network of ideas into which new facts should be fitted (paradigm 1). For example, computer science is mostly working under what we can call the 'information-theory paradigm', which says that the information in a storage system such as a computer or a book is a series of symbols which can be regarded as instructions or descriptions, and can be manipulated according to other symbolic instructions and translated into other symbols for our convenience. This may seem obvious, but only because we have been using this paradigm since the mid-nineteenth century. It would have seemed bizarre to Isaac Newton, and is being viewed with some suspicion by connectionists today because of its emphasis on symbols and their manipulation.

The second meaning (paradigm 2) relates to the first. Paradigms 1 are characterized by exemplary experiments, which themselves are called 'paradigms'. These illustrate key ideas in the paradigm 1 in some particularly novel or revealing way. In computer science two of the paradigms 2 are the Babbage machine, the mechanical computer designed by Charles Babbage in the late nineteenth century that is widely considered a precursor of today's electronic versions, and the Turing machine. They are 'experiments' to show, respectively, that any computation can be reduced to discrete instructions in a machine, and that all digital computers are equivalent.

Thus paradigm 2 is a specific experiment, paradigm 1 is a whole collection of ideas, experimental results and theories which make sense of the paradigm 2 experiments, and which are in turn bolstered by them.

Paradigms 2 need not actually *work*. The Babbage machine certainly did not: it was never even built. It was used as an example of an approach to a problem.

Like 'syndrome', 'chemistry' and other technical terms, 'paradigm' has been abused. Feel superior to people who use it as a synonym for:

1. *Example*   Only a few, key examples are paradigms 2
2. *Theory*   A whole lot of theories and key examples *may* make up a paradigm. One theory makes as much of a paradigm as one swallow makes a meal.
3. *Idea or hypothesis*   As above.
4. *Way of looking at things*   A paradigm is much more than *just* a viewpoint. The correct synonym here is 'prejudice'.
5. *My latest product*   The most common use. Enough said.

PARALLEL INFERENCE MACHINE

Hardware

The parallel inference machine has been under development as the central component of the Japanese fifth-generation computer. It is to be a parallel computer with 1000 processors, grouped into clusters which share common memory, each cluster communicating with other clusters via a network organized by another cluster of processors. This is to make the machine faster, because the main processors do not spend time passing information which they themselves do not require.

The processors are designed to be easy to program for logical and symbolic operations (as a Lisp chip is), rather than being centred around numerical abilities. The PIM will also allow easy representation of uncertain data.

A precursor of the PIM, the PSI (personal sequential inference machine), works as a PC version of the PIM, providing inference and logical power at a personal computer level. The PSI is not a parallel computer, but the processor used in it is similar to that which will form the basis of the PIM.

New languages and operating systems are also being developed for the PIM and PSI.

Unlike traditional computers, where the computer's speed is measured in the number of arithmetic operations it can perform per second, the PIM's performance (and that of other potential AI-specific machines) is usually quoted in LIPS (logical inferences per second) or KLIPS (kilo = thousand).

PARALLEL PROCESSING

Hardware

Parallel processing means running programs which perform more than one operation at a time. Conventional computers perform operations one after the other (*serial* or sequential).

There are four flavours of parallel processing:

1. vector processing;
2. array processing;
3. distributed processing;
4. neural-net processing;

In *vector processing*, a number of processors perform one operation on one data element at a time, as in Cray computers. The operation (multiplying two elements of a matrix together, say) is split into a series of simple steps, and each processor handles one step, thus working on a different part of the same calculation. Thus the processors are operating in parallel, performing different operations on the same data. Vector processors are often used as 'add-ons' for conventional processors.

In *array processing*, the computer contains a number of processors which perform identical operations on different data. Suppose I wanted to add 17 to 64 different numbers. An array processor would tell its processors to add 17 to the next number they received, and then feed one number to each processor. This approach is also called SIMD (single instruction, multiple data). The ICL DAP (Distributed Array Processor) was an array-processing machine, with four processors.

Array and vector processing are fairly similar, and are used to solve similar types of problem.

Distributed processing occurs when different processors can do different things, although still working in concert on one overall problem. It is also called multiple instruction, multiple data (MIMD) programming. Transputers and the *Connection Machine* are MIMD machines.

166

Other terms are: *common memory processors*, in which a number of processors share access to the same memory (vector processors are examples); and *distributed memory*, in which each processor has its own chunk of memory and communicates with other processors through more constrained communication links (distributed processors are of this type).

In these sorts of parallel processing, there is one master controller that programs the processors and feeds them their data. This is not so in the last class of parallel processing, *neural net processing*. This is a form of distributed processing, but is radically different from conventional processing, in that there is no central controller, and often no program.

Parallel processing is of interest to AI for two reasons. First, the solution of some AI problems requires enormous amounts of computer time. If that time can be 'telescoped' into a parallel-processing solution, a lot of run time can be saved. Second, some problems are better solved by parallel methods. For example, vision is an activity in which an entire image has to be processed at once, and how you interpret one part depends on how you interpret another. The way you identify a collection of fuzzy lines, say, depends on whether the are attached to the back of a dog or the end of a stick, but the way you identify the dog depends on whether you can see its tail. This is efficiently processed in parallel. Some more formal problems, like the *travelling salesman problem* for example, are also like this: they are said to have *high connectivity*.

See also: Connectionism, Distributed processing, Neural nets

PARSER

NLP

In natural-language processing, a parser is a program which, given a sentence and a *grammar*, can test whether the sentence is one of those described by that grammar. Sentences which 'pass the test' (are recognized to conform to an acceptable sentence structure) may be converted further into a *parse tree* (see below).

A grammar, in the context of a parser, refers to a set of rules which specify how certain symbols may legitimately be combined. A grammar for describing insults, for example, tells you exactly how an 'insult' may be expressed, as follows.

1. An ⟨insult⟩ is a ⟨suggested action⟩ followed by the word YOU and by a ⟨rude name⟩.
2. A ⟨suggested action⟩ is GO JUMP IN THE LAKE or GET LOST.
3. A ⟨rude name⟩ is an ⟨adjective⟩ followed by FAT PIG or FILTHY BEAST.
4. An ⟨adjective⟩ is HORRID or SILLY

This gives

   Get lost you silly fat pig
   Go jump in the lake you horrid filthy beast

as example sentences.

A parser for this grammar will consist of a program which scans a sentence and tests that it has the right parts in the right order to be classed as an insult.

Some parsers analyse a sentence by starting with the most general structure (the sentence) and then testing for finer and finer components. These are the *top-down parsers*. In the insult grammar above, a parser might begin by 'thinking':

'Is this list of words I've been given an ⟨insult⟩?'

which in turn sparks off:

'Is there a ⟨suggested action⟩'?
'Is there a ⟨rude name⟩'?

Accordingly, the parser sees if the individual English words it has been given correspond to adjectives and rude names allowed.

A *bottom-up* parser works the other way round. It uses the rules 'backwards'. First it looks at the words given and tries to see what parts of speech they are. Then it puts two and two together and discovers that the words include a ⟨suggested action⟩, a YOU and a ⟨rude name⟩. They therefore constitute an ⟨insult⟩.

During the course of parsing an insult, the program may generate a parse tree. This is a representation of the syntactic form of the insult. For example:

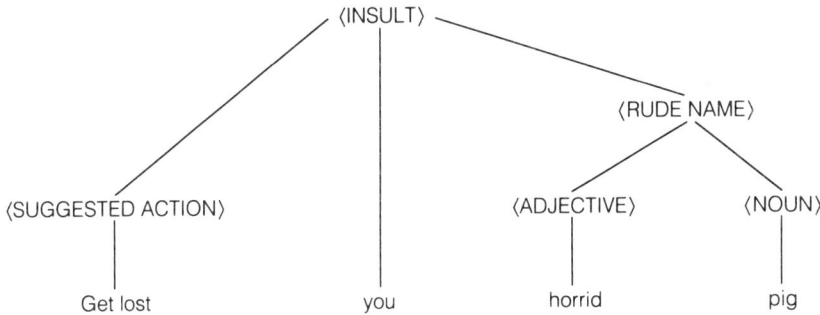

Parsing sentences in terms of their syntax (the order of words they contain) has its limitations. Much harder, but more effective, is to analyse a sentence in terms of what it means. In the 1970s, a whole class of parsers were developed which classified words according to the roles they played in the sentence, sometimes in quite a sophisticated way. For example, using the ideas of conceptual dependency theory, which proposes that only a dozen or so primitive acts represent events and causal sequences of events, a parser might convert the sentence

Eleanor gave Thomas the teddy bear

into a representation that spelt out who gave, who received, what was given, who liked whom and so on.

PERCEPTRON

Neural nets

A perceptron is the name of a simple, two-layer neural-net computer, which models the workings of the retina of the eye. Perceptrons were the subject of research in the late 1950s and early 1960s. They could be trained to recognize patterns, something conventional computers find hard to do.

However, Minsky and Papert showed that there are classes of problem which perceptrons cannot solve in principle. They generalized this conclusion to all neural nets, and concluded that they would not make a major contribution to computing. The recent renewed interest in neural-net models of computation is due to the widespread realization that this generalization was wrong, and does not hold for neural nets with 'hidden layers'.

See also: Neural net

PLANNING

Search

AI addresses many problems in the planning of tasks for which there are several ways of proceeding, such as stacking boxes in a factory. Planning programs create detailed schemes of how to achieve some specified end state. It is no trivial matter to plan tasks in such a way that each action takes place at the right time and place, and that one task does not interfere with another.

Planning systems have to be able to reason about the constraints on their subject matter, about causality, and about strategies. As a practical output the system aims to tell the user the extent to which an action fits in with an existing plan, or what choices she has in performing a task.

Planning programs were tried out on the *blocks world*, where a target state could be described unambiguously, and the program had complete knowledge about the 'world'. SHRDLU, the natural-language program, contained a planner to enable the computer to work out how to move from the current situation to the one the user desired. Some practical applications, such as stacking boxes in automated warehouse systems, are very similar to this blocks-world application.

Planning in this sense has been applied primarily to robot control. However, it has also been used in planning industrial projects, journeys, job scheduling, defence, satellite missions and scientific experiments, with varying success.

PRAGMATICS

NLP

Pragmatics, as a term used in natural-language processing, is the study of how people express what they really mean. If you say to someone: 'You fat pig!', this can be analysed at various levels:

1. the words themselves (you, fat and pig);
2. the grammatical organization of words in the sentence (fat is an adjective, pig is a noun);
3. the semantics of the sentence: the ideas it contains (the person is a fat pig);
4. the concepts behind and governing that sentence (insult, speaker intends to attack).

To understand 'You fat pig!' pragmatically, an NLP system requires not merely knowledge about English grammar and vocabulary, but a lot of information about the world in general. This kind of knowledge is, of course, very hard to put 'inside a computer'.

See also: Natural-language processing

PREDICATE

Logic

A predicate is a term derived originally from mathematical logic. It is an idea used widely in programming languages for AI applications.

A predicate is a function whose value may be either TRUE or FALSE. For example, here is a question written in Prolog:

?likes (bears, honey)

What this amounts to is this:

Does the predicate 'likes' hold true or false for the individuals bears and honey?

In Lisp, some functions return a value TRUE or FALSE and, as such, are predicates. For example, take the predicate LESSTHAN. It takes two numbers and compares them. If the first is smaller than the second, the predicate is satisfied and Lisp returns the value T (for true); otherwise LISP returns the value NIL (for false).

All Prolog rules are predicates (although they are often not used as such).

See also: Prolog, Logic programming

PREDICATE CALCULUS

Logic

Predicate calculus is a way of writing and manipulating ideas about the world with the precision of a mathematical formula. As an example of first-order logic, predicate calculus is more complicated than its relation, propositional calculus.

To understand predicate calculus, first consider propositional calculus and its limitations. This is a method for calculating whether simple statements are true or false. In propositional calculus, simple true-or-false statements form the foundations of your knowledge, and from them other statements may be deduced as being true or false.

By using the *propositional connectives* (see the entry on *propositional calculus*), strings of simple statements can be assembled to give a compound statement structure:

John likes treacle AND John likes honey AND John has a car.

However, even with compound statements, the emphasis is still on the truth or falsehood of the component parts: there are limitations to what the logic of propositional calculus allows you to express. An obvious limitation is that you are not allowed to write rules or theorems. This is because you cannot use quantifiers. You cannot say that, 'for all' or 'for a certain class of items', such and such is the case. For example, you cannot say:

All people called John like treacle.

Predicate calculus *does* allow the use of variables *and* quantifiers. With the use of propositional connectives to construct 'sentences' of corrected formulated logic, many ideas can be expressed.

For example:

∀ x. Cat (x) → Has Whiskers (x).

For any object x in the world, if x is a cat, then x has whiskers. ∀ is the *universal quantifier*, which specifies that any proposition will be true for any individuals whose names are substituted for the variable.

x. ∃ Cat (x) and Black (x) and Greedy (x).

There is an x which is a cat that is black and greedy.

∃ is the *existential variable*, which specifies that certain individuals exist for which the proposition will be true.

Predicate calculus has been popular with logicians, but if you try to translate real-life ideas into it, the expressions you get are extremely long and incomprehensible. For this reason, predicate calculus is rarely used 'neat'. However, it has formed the internal basis of various AI systems that use logic to represent knowledge. Examples are the STRIPS system and logic-programming languages such as Prolog.

See also: Propositional calculus

PRIMAL SKETCH

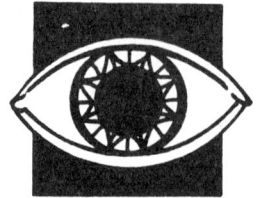

Vision

This is the first recognition state of image processing in some computer vision systems. A primal sketch is a cartoon-like drawing in which the image has been reduced to a line drawing composed of 'edges' derived directly from image data. Primal sketches come in two sorts, as follows.

1. *Raw primal sketch*. This is the collection of edges that the vision system detects in the initial image. It looks a bit like a cartoon, but has a lot of 'erroneous' lines because of 'noise' in the signal.
2. *Full primal sketch*. This is the raw primal sketch after the erroneous lines have been removed, and only those that belong to the 'real' image remain. The trick here is to decide what is 'real' image and what is noise. The usual criterion is that a bit of noise will appear as an isolated edge in the middle of nowhere, while a real edge will join up with a lot of other edges. This is hard to achieve for complex images.

Primal images are part of the 'traditional' school of computer vision deriving from the work of David Marr. They play no role in the connectionist theories of vision, in which the overall pattern of light and dark is related to the objects in the field of view, and the picture is not built up from small local features to larger-scale objects.

In some vision systems, the input data are pre-processed before the edge-detection step by removing some of the visual 'noise'. This usually involves removing isolated points of light in a dark area, or of dark in a light area.

PROCEDURAL PROGRAMMING LANGUAGE

Logic

A procedural programming language consists of a series of procedures or actions usually called 'statements' or 'commands'. For example:

Multiply X by Y.
Test to see if this is grammatically correct.
Add this word to this list.

This is in contrast to a *declarative programming language*, in which a program consists of a number of factual statements from which conclusions are inferred as programs are run.

See also: Declarative programming language

PROCESS

General
computer
term

In computer terminology, a process is a single logical chain of operations. Thus a single session at the terminal or with a microcomputer might be a process: you start, load a file into memory, and run a program, doing one thing after another. Separate processes only communicate with each other through well-defined channels, typically by passing messages of defined structure.

See also: Concurrency

PRODUCTION RULE

Prog.
techniques

The term 'production rule' is used fairly generally in AI to cover a number of systems of knowledge representation. A production rule consists of a condition and action pair. For example:

If chances of explosion greater than 1 in a million...

then ... add 'highly dangerous' to list
of possible consequences.

A production rule is said to have a 'left-hand side' and a 'right-hand side'. Once the conditions on the left-hand side have been met, then the rule is said to 'fire' and the appropriate action is carried out.

The expert system MYCIN is famous for its use of production rules. MYCIN deals with diseases of the blood. As the (simplified) rule below demonstrates, a MYCIN production rule may be written in Lisp. The rule consists of a premise (the conditions for firing) and an action to take when the rule is fired.

```
PREMISE:   (AND (SAME CONTEXT SITE BLOOD)
                (SAME CONTEXT STAIN GRAM_NEGATIVE)
                (SAME CONTEXT MORPHOLOGY ROD))
ACTION:    (CONCLUDE (CONTEXT IDENTITY ECOLI TALLY 0.6))
```

When the rule is fired (which happens when the site of the disease is the blood, the bacterium test gram-negative and the bacterium is rod-shaped to look at), the 'context' (CONTEXT) list is updated with new information. In this case, the identity of the bacterium is added to the list together with some indication of how likely it is that the identity is correct.

Thus the context list represents the patient profile, which changes as new tests on his or her blood are performed.

By using a context list, production rules maintain independence from each other. If production rules intermesh, for example:

A if B and C
C if D and E
B if F and H

editing the system becomes much more tricky, particularly if several hundred rules are involved.

Since many production rules are used in a *forward-chaining* expert system, a rule interpreter is needed to apply rules in the right order. A rule interpreter might use ideas as follows.

1. Look at all rules and if the conditions for any rule are met, fire that rule.
2. Deactivate any rules which, when fired, would duplicate items already on the context list.

See also: Meta-rule, Knowledge base

PROLOG

Prog.
techniques

Prolog is a programming language based on ideas taken from mathematical logic (see *logic programming*).

In logic, facts are stated simply and formally so that they can form the basis of logical argument. From a set of facts correctly phrased, a logician can use certain logical methods to 'infer' new facts from old:

Eleanor likes peanut butter sandwiches
If Eleanor likes something, Eleanor eats it
Eleanor eats peanut butter sandwiches

Prolog was developed by logicians interested in *automated inference*, in which the computer essentially becomes the logician, examining facts listed in program form.

The kind of inference which proved especially easy to automate was *SL resolution*, devised in 1972 by the logician Bob Kowalski. SL resolution inferred facts from the horn clause sub-set of a logic called *predicate calculus*. SL resolution was developed by Colmerauer into Prolog.

The classic demonstration of Prolog involves relationships amongst people. Take the following:

    manager_of (adam, clare)
    manager_of (richard, eleanor)

which mean:

    Adam is the manager of Clare.
    Richard is the manager of Eleanor.

Whereas these are specific statements of fact, Prolog can also be used to make statements more general:

likes (X,Y) :- manager_of (X,Y)

This means that, if there are two people called X and Y, then X likes Y if X is the manager of Y. Now, if we ask Prolog the question:

? likes (adam, clare)

essentially:

Does Adam like Clare?

Prolog can deduce that, since Adam is the manager of Clare, then Adam must also like her. Other programming languages can do this sort of thing of course, but not nearly so neatly.

But how does Prolog differ from conventional programming languages? The conventional programmer thinks in terms of algorithms: step-wise instructions to perform certain tasks. Programmers using Prolog concentrate on defining what formal relationships are true in the problem (who is the manager of whom, who likes whom etc.) and what formal relationships hold true in the desired solution. As a result, programming in Prolog involves thinking very methodically and being extremely finicky.

The logical relationships which form the essence of a program can be rather abstract and hard to grasp. For this reason, textbooks on Prolog and logic programming often quote exhaustive examples of relationships between members of family trees rather than real programming examples. Such relationships are more down to earth and easier to understand, yet have parallels in true logic programming.

An example of a rather difficult, yet widely used idea in Prolog, is the APPEND predicate. This defines explicitly and completely what is logically involved in joining two lists together. At first sight trivial, this task proves more interesting than at first imagined. See *logic programming.*

See also: Logic programming

PROPOSITIONAL CALCULUS

Logic

Computational logic, which involves performing logical reasoning with a computer, is traditionally known as 'symbolic logic' or 'mathematical logic'. It includes propositional calculus and the more complicated *predicate calculus*. Predicate calculus forms the basis of logic-programming languages which are often used for AI applications. Propositional calculus is not used as such, but is a run-up to predicate calculus.

Propositional calculus centres around the idea of an atomic statement, a fundamental statement called a 'proposition', to which we may give a value either TRUE or FALSE. For example:

Proposition s	2 plus 2 are 4	TRUE
Proposition p	Harry has ginger hair	FALSE
Proposition q	I have a cold	TRUE

On their own, propositions are not very useful. However, the scope of what they can express is increased by the use of propositional connectives. These are:

NOT;
AND;
OR;
IMPLIES.

By combining propositions in many different ways, whole sentences of propositional logic may be built:

(p AND (p IMPLIES q)) IMPLIES q.

Propositional sentences are written using letters to represent the propositions, and parentheses are used just as in mathematics. Indeed the treatment of propositions is very much a mathematical one, with no respect for the real-life meaning behind individual statements.

The behaviour of the propositional connectives is captured in a diagram called a *truth table*. This allows you to see at a glance the effect of the propositional connective:

Truth table for OR

p	q	(p OR q)
T	F	T
T	T	T
F	T	T
F	F	F

From this you can see that, for example, if propositions *p* and *q* are true, then the proposition (p OR q) is true also.

We have outlined the type of statement that propositional calculus allows, but how can statements of this kind be used?

Propositional calculus does not allow rules to be used to process propositions, in the same way that predicate calculus does, for example. However, simple inferences can be made by virtue of the propositional connectives. For example, take *modus ponens* (see *Deduction*), an inference method summed up as follows:

(p AND (p IMPLIES q)) IMPLIES q

or: if we know that the truth of p implies q, and we know that p is true, then q is also true. We can sum up this argument form as follows:

p	premis
p implies q	premis
q	conclusion

An example of *modus ponens* is:

It is cold
If it is cold then I must put my coat on
I must put my coat on

184

This sounds trivial, but the point is that it is mathematically correct and logically sound. Propositional logic uses a large number of argument forms, all of which can be verified by using truth tables.

PROTOCOL

General
computer
term

In robotics (and many other things, such as DIY), a protocol is a description of how something is done, like a recipe. The amount of detail in the protocol depends on who it is meant for: a robot needs more detail than a human, for whom 'pick up spanner' can be one instruction. A robot can be 'taught' such a protocol by being taken through it movement by movement (this type of teaching is called *lead-through*), or can be pre-programmed with the necessary steps.

A related meaning is found in data communication, where a protocol is a procedure and a set of data formats for establishing a link and transferring data between machines. There are a wide range of detailed protocols to do this.

In knowledge acquisition, a protocol is a written description of what someone actually does while they are performing an action, including a verbal description of what they are thinking while they solve a problem. This includes all the 'ums' and 'ers', as well as dead-ends and apparent non-sequiturs, as these might prove to be important parts of the logical process, ruling out some option which otherwise looked quite promising. Thus the protocol in this second sense is usually much more rambling than in the first sense.

See also: Knowledge elicitation

186

RAPID PROTOTYPING

Prog.
techniques

The process of designing an expert system is extremely complicated. There are questions about what the expert system should 'know', what the interface should look like, and so on. These points are covered under *knowledge engineering*.

A rapid prototype is a system rigged up quickly so that the client can see what is envisaged. Although the system gives the flavour of the real product, the knowledge base may be incomplete and the system may not make optimal use of the hardware available. As a result the prototype may run rather slowly, use memory inefficiently, and have a relatively shallow knowledge of the domain. A finely tuned expert system takes so long to build that it is worth making doubly sure you are on the right track before you go too far.

See also: Experimental system

RECURSION

Prog.
techniques

Suppose you wanted to explain to someone who their relatives were; you might answer 'they are your parents and the relatives of your parents'. All very well, but for those who don't actually know what 'relatives' means in the first place, not very enlightening. This is because the explanation relies on the very concept being defined: the explanation is viciously circular. In the language of mathematics, you have given a *recursive definition.*

In mathematics and in certain types of programming, recursive definitions can be very useful. The classic demonstration of recursion in *logic programming* gets the computer to reason about relationships within a family tree. It turns out that the logic involved in manipulating such relationships has many parallels in real logic-programming applications, and that this, rather than the lack of originality on the part of the authors, explains why the same kind of example crops up again and again.

The following is a definition for the relation 'is an ancestor of':

1. X is an ancestor of Y if
    X is a parent of Y
2. X is an ancestor of Y if
    X is a parent of Z and
    Z is an ancestor of Y

If you think through this definition, you first pin-point your parents as your ancestors. Then you cite the parents of your parents: your grandparents, and then your great grandparents, then your great great grandparents and so on.

The recursive rule 2 does the trick of discovering every ancestor: the family tree is searched from the root to the tips of its branches where the more distant ancestors lie. The non-recursive rule (rule 1) halts procedures once the most distant ancestors have been discovered.

A very common application of recursion in logic programming is the APPEND predicate. This specifies what is logically involved when you join together two lists of words or symbols. If you wanted to join the words 'the cat' to 'sat on the mat', you could arrange it so that the APPEND predicate would be satisfied only when the two lists of words were correctly strung together to give the complete sentence.

Lisp is a *functional computer language*: it takes numbers, words, names or other symbols and processes them with 'functions'. Quite often, when defining a new function, the programmer will use the very function being defined in the definition. In other words, the function may have a recursive feature.

The example below demonstrates a recursive function in the functional language Hope. This involves the idea of 'factorials': the product of all the positive numbers from 1 up to and including a given number. The factorial of 5 is $1 \times 2 \times 3 \times 4 \times 5$.

```
dec factorial: num  →  num;
    factorial (n)
        ⇐ if n = 1
              then 1
              else factorial (n - 1) *n
```

If $n = 5$, its factorial is five times the factorial of $(5 - 1)$ (the last line in the program): so much is clear. However, this definition necessitates the discovery of the factorial of $(5 - 1)$, in other words, the factorial of 4. Thus we need to go full circle through the program again, and then twice more, discovering the factorial of 4, 3, and 2 in turn. The non-recursive part of the program 'if n = 1 then 1' halts the procedure when n has reached a value of 1.

REWRITE RULE

Prog.
techniques

A rewrite rule is a programming technique with a range of applications. It is a rule which states that whenever a program reads in something, it replaces it with something else. Thus a rewrite rule that said 'Replace COW by PIG' would input the sentence

The cow jumped over the moon

and output the sentence

The pig jumped over the moon.

This has two general uses, in automata and in grammar. Many of the simple, theoretical computers called *automata* operate on rewrite rules, in that they input a string of characters from a 'tape' and output an altered string to the same tape.

The *grammar* of some (theoretical) languages, specifically context-free languages, may be described as a series of rewrite rules. Here we start off with a symbol for our sentence, S. Our parser has a rule: Rewrite S by N-V, where N is noun phrase and V is a verb phrase. It also has a rule 'Rewrite N with Article-Noun', so the parser rewrites the sentence Article-Noun-V and so on. Thus it ends up with a vastly expanded version of the symbol S. This is just another way of describing the parsing process, but has implications for what the computer is actually doing.

Functional languages may also be processed in this way. The function 'factorial' may be processed as a series of rewrite rules thus:

Factorial (3) rewrites to
3 * factorial (2) which rewrites to

190

3 * 2 * factorial (1) which rewrites to
3 * 2 * 1 which is
6

See also: Grammar

RISC

Hardware

RISC stands for reduced instruction set computer, a recent approach to making computers substantially faster. The limit of how fast a computer can operate is how fast its chips can perform their basic operations (machine instructions or machine code). The complete collection of all basic instructions is called the computer's 'instruction set'. Programs written in higher-level languages like Fortran and Lisp have to be translated into machine instructions by a compiler before the computer can 'run' them.

Computer designers have tended to put complicated instructions in their computer's instruction set, sometimes combining a number of basic steps into one instruction, to reduce the work that compilers and interpreters have to do and hence, in theory, make them faster. However, these complicated instructions reduce the efficiency of the CPU as a whole. As most compilers usually only use a fraction of the machine-code commands at their disposal, computer designers came up with a reduced instruction set computer with many fewer machine-code commands, but those operating much faster. RISCs operate much faster for relatively simple programs.

Coming soon is the MISC: the minuscule instruction set computer. This will have only one machine-code instruction, and it will be blindingly fast, as soon as someone can figure out what the instruction should be.

ROBOTICS

Hardware

Robotics is the construction and programming of robots, which these days means complex, flexible, programmable machines of any shape or size. The construction and engineering details are not discussed here. However, the programming often uses AI techniques, particularly in vision systems (to tell the robot where an object is) and in planning (to tell the robot how and when to move it somewhere else).

SCRIPT

NLP

A script is a means of representing and organizing the information obtained from some source: a newspaper article, for example. Scripts find their basis in psychology. Psychologists have pointed out that people interpret new situations in the light of previous experience. When you visit a supermarket, for instance, you have a vision of what to expect: supermarket trolleys at the entrance, shelves filled with items of food, check-out counters and so on. Equally, you expect certain sequences of events to take place: you expect to go round the shelves filling your trolley up and to queue at the check-out and pay. Scripts use this idea of expectation to interpret information. A script is a schema that deals with stereotyped activities.

Imagine a computer that scans newspaper articles for information relating to a particular subject. The computer uses techniques from natural-language processing (see *natural-language processing* and *parser*) to break down sentences into their component parts, and then extracts some degree of meaning from the article by filling in a script. Articles on food poisoning, for example, are all likely to contain information on who, where and how people were poisoned. The script might therefore have slots for these as follows:

Who was poisoned: Mr Black and 16 friends

Where: Yummo Food café

How: not known

Symptoms: violent stomach upsets four hours after eating

Action: café to re-house pet pig outside

See also: Frame

SEARCH

Search

Search is the general name given to finding the answer to a problem, given a large number of possible routes to the solution.

Suppose you are faced with a bunch of keys and wonder which one opens your door. Most people try each key at random. They then become infuriated because they lose track of which keys they have tried. A few people try one key after another in a methodical way, putting aside the wrong keys until they find the one that works.

In AI, the process of search requires such methodical thinking. A programmer needs to think carefully about how to represent the initial situation at the start of the problem, the desired solution to the problem, and the stages in between. He also needs to tell the computer which moves are allowed to get from one intermediate stage in solving the problem to another.

Some of the earliest methods for representing the different stages in solving problems involved 'state graphs'. These show the intermediate stages in solving a problem as a number of 'states'. Arranged in a net-like structure, movement from one state to another is accomplished by the use of 'operators'. A solution is a path from the initial state to the final state. An example of a state graph is given in the entry *game tree*. The collection of all the points ('nodes') on a state graph is sometimes called the 'search space'.

A search tree shows which paths in a state graph have been explored. The search begins at the initial node of the state graph and the search tree grows as the various branches are explored. By applying all the possible operators to a given state, you can generate all the successors of a give node.

For many problems, the search space is unmanageably large: the number of successors for any given node may be enormous. Bear in mind that the computer can only see a tiny portion of the search tree at a time. There is no way that it can intelligently scan the whole tree at once and see the answer to a problem in the way that a person might. The computer needs to adopt some method of exploring nodes systematically one by one, some way of assessing whether nodes encountered are on the way to the solution to the problem, and some way of making sure that not too much information has to be held in memory at any one time.

Systematic searching classically proceeds by depth-first or breadth-first search. In *depth-first search*, the computer chooses a branch of the tree and investigates every node right to the tip of the branch before backing up and trying another branch. *Breadth-first search* involves looking at level after level within the search tree.

But, although computers may search very fast through a search tree, exhaustive unguided search is often not efficient enough. Heuristics (rules of thumb which are used to assign values to nodes to indicate how 'useful' they are) are often used to guide search. For example, you might decide, in the search for the station Finchley Road on a train map, that stations north of your present position in the network are good ones to aim for. You apply the heuristic 'nodes north of my present position are good'. You might be wrong of course, but the heuristic does serve to narrow down your options.

Certain algorithms ensure that any route the computer finally picks between a starting node and a solution node represents the minimum-cost path. A well-known one is the A^T algorithm (algorithm for trees). This uses the idea of associating with every node n, a number g which is the total cost of the path from the top node to node n.

Nodes with the lowest value of n are favoured as the computer decides which of many nodes to investigate initially. As search progresses down the tree, nodes with low values of g are always selected for expansion and their successors generated. Nodes with unfavourable values are rejected and not expanded. It can be proved that the A^T algorithm will always find the minimum-cost path.

Interest in search was at its height in the 1970s; the focus today is more on knowledge and how to represent it.

SEGMENTATION

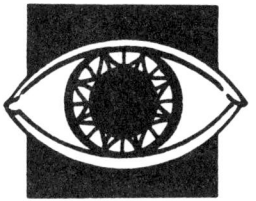

Vision

Segmentation is a term used in vision research to describe how the computer analyses an object by breaking it up into meaningful components. Segmentation can be performed at two levels on an image.

At the lower level, an image can be segmented into *regions* of different shade or texture. This is a process that can be performed in parallel with forming a *primal sketch*, and which provides some fairly simple information about the number and, potentially, orientation of planes in the image. In combination with edge data, the regions so defined can then be examined to see whether they correspond to flat planes, shadows etc.

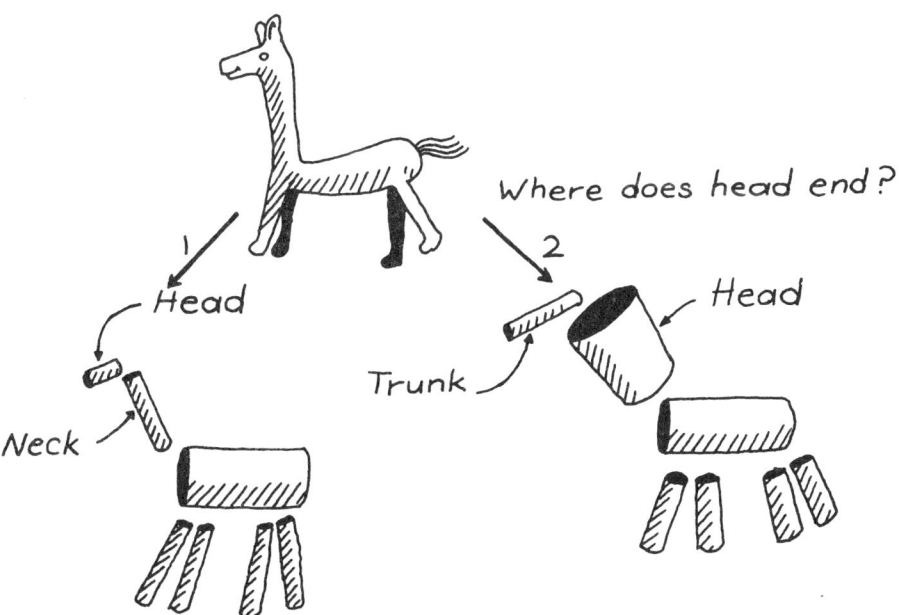

At a higher level, segmentation is concerned with finding the *boundaries* between sections of an object, and hence what that object is. For example, an elephant may be defined as an animal with a trunk, but unless the computer can correctly segment the animal it is detecting into nose-head-neck-body, it will be confused between elephants and giraffes. Thus this (much harder) version of the segmentation problem is about how to break up an object which looks like a complicated blob into segments that can be used for identification.

Usually objects are segmented into *generalized cylinders*. A cylinder is the shape swept out by a circle it moves in a straight line through the air. A generalized cylinder is the space swept out by any shape as it moves along any line in the air. Thus an elephant is approximated by a large cylinder labelled 'body' with various cylinders protruding from it labelled head, legs etc. This simple description can then be stored in some form of database as a graph or list. Increasing detail can be added by adding more, smaller, cylinders. The problem comes in deciding the junctions between the cylinders. Incorrect decisions result in shooting a giraffe for its tusks. There are heuristic rules to segment pictures, but no general method: how we do it probably depends in part on experience and in part on the neural connections in our brains.

See also: Texture

SEMANTIC NET

Prog.
techniques

A semantic net is a way of formally representing concepts and the relationships between them. Semantic nets were introduced by Quillian in 1969 as an alternative structural form to the database, and heralded a period of interest in the representation of meaning in natural language.

A semantic net is a graph in which each simple concept is represented as a node, and the relationships between concepts are represented as arcs. For example, a semantic net describing features of insects might look like this:

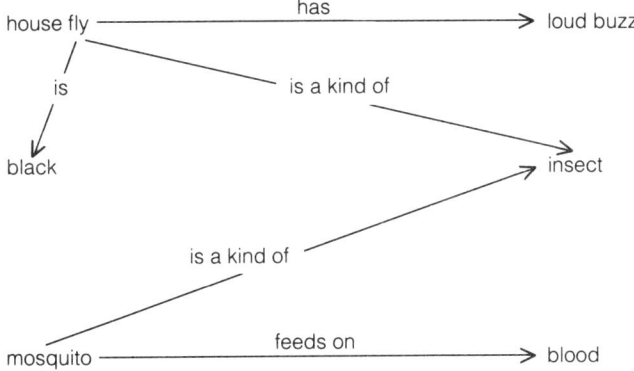

What would this look like as a computer program? A semantic net is merely a description of information and not a program. To make a workable program out of a semantic net, an entirely separate collection of rules is needed to enable the computer to use the facts it posesses. For example, if we add:

insect is a house fly if it has a loud buzz and is black;
insect is a mosquito if it feeds on blood;

then our semantic net becomes more than just a collection of facts about insects and their features: it allows us to query the database to see if an expression we give it is supported by the information in the database. In other words, the semantic net then allows us to test if a given fact is 'true'.

See also: Knowledge base, Semantics

SEMANTICS

NLP

Semantics refers to the meaning of language. This is in contrast to its syntax, which merely specifies the sequential arrangement of words in a sentence, as allowed by the rules of *grammar*.

Take the sentence:

The apple tasted blue.

Although syntactically correct, it is semantically wrong: it conforms to English grammar, yet it is nonsense.

In AI, the problem of meaning poses a serious barrier to the success of systems that can understand natural language. Although we can talk about what something means in an informal sense, we do so with a wealth of common sense and experience to help us. Even if you give a computer the dictionary meaning of each word in a paragraph of text, the ideas behind the text may remain completely elusive. The meaning of a paragraph is more than the sum of its parts.

Some AI researchers are optimistic that parallel processing and neural-net technology will help. Maybe architectures like these will allow computers to assess thousands of different meanings in parallel at once, to see which one makes sense in its context.

See also: Syntax, Pragmatics

201

SERIAL

General
computer
term

A serial or sequential computer is one that performs its instructions one at a time. 'Von Neuman machines', i.e. 'normal' computers like most commercial computers, are serial, as are all mini- and microcomputers. The alternatives to serial processing are *parallel processing* and *distributed processing*.

See also: Parallel processing, Neural nets

SILICON RETINA

Hardware

This is a piece of research hardware which performs pattern analysis on images. The retina is the layer of nerve cells, lining the eyeball, that detect light. It carries out basic processing functions on the image, such as edge detection. Carver Mead has built a semiconductor analogue of this neural layer, called the silicon retina, which replicates many of the functions of the biological retina by duplicating many aspects of its organization and dynamics. This neural-net chip can be used for pre-processing an image, and is a key example of the practical use of neural nets for performing pattern processing, massively parallel tasks at which conventional computers are relatively inefficient.

See also: Neural nets

SIMULATION V EMULATION

Theory/
philosophy

One of the main criticisms of AI is that it produces results that are not actually 'intelligent', but only look as if they are. In other words, AI programs do not emulate human activities, but only simulate them. The classic simulation program was ELIZA, which searched for key symbols (words) in an input string and output some other string in accordance with the input. The result could look very like a conversation, but meant nothing to the computer; there was no 'understanding' of the question in the program, only manipulation of key symbols.

The thesis that all rules-based systems are merely simulating a human activity is put forward most eloquently by John Searle with his *Chinese room* analogy of AI. The criticism is probably most powerful when applied to traditional computer vision systems, which have few obvious connections with our visual processing (and work poorly anyway); it is less powerful for expert systems. The latter operate rules which have been defined with the help of the experts themselves as being the way *they* think. Of course, this is not necessarily a good representation of how they *do* think: rather, it is a description of the conscious processes which the experts can formalize. This leaves out much of their tacit knowledge, which expert systems may only simulate. The argument is probably weakest when applied to neural nets.

See also: Chinese room

SPEECH SYNTHESIS

General AI
term

Speech synthesis is the computer generation of spoken output from non-acoustic, coded input (usually 'printed' words). Unlike many AI applications, it is very successful.

Most speech-synthesis systems take a text in a given language and generate a voice version of it. This is not trivial, and lots of rules, most of them quite arbitrary, have to be applied to make sure that words which look the same but are pronounced differently come out right. (The standard test sentence for this is 'The rough wind brought the bough down': can the machine remember that rOUGH, brOUGHt and bOUGH sound quite different, while BOUGH and DOWN sound almost the same?) Good systems also inflect sentences: the quaint, droning, monotone whine of so many computers in television science fiction does not actually emerge from real programs.

STRONG KNOWLEDGE/ WEAK KNOWLEDGE

General AI
term

Strong knowledge is specific and highly sophisticated knowledge about the domain. In chess, strong knowledge is the kind of knowledge a grand master has. It consists of strategies, involving the recognition of classic trends and situations. It does not involve 'rules of thumb' applicable to a wide range of board positions, but rather the recognition of specific sequences of moves and their consequences.

Weak knowledge, by contrast, is the sort of knowledge a novice chess player might have. Weak knowledge consists of heuristics: rules of thumb to apply to decide which of many different possible moves is the best. Whilst weak knowledge can be picked up fairly quickly, strong knowledge takes time to acquire.

SYMBOLIC EXPRESSION

General
computer
term

A symbolic expression is any expression that uses symbols instead of actual numbers, letters, words or whatever. Thus

2 * 3

is an arithmetic expression, because it expresses something in arithmetic language. If we wanted a more general expression, we would use symbols

x * *y*

where *x* and *y* are symbols standing for numbers, but not actually numbers themselves. (Of course, '2' and '3' are symbols as well, standing for 'two somethings' and 'three somethings'). A related term is *symbolic computation*. The first expression above is actually a computation: we are computing 2 times 3. The expression below it is a symbolic version of it, i.e. a symbolic computation. At school this is called *algebra*, and thus symbolic computation is indeed computer algebra.

SYMBOLIC PROGRAMMING LANGUAGE

General AI term

Computer languages such as Fortran and Basic are particularly adept at doing arithmetic. The same languages are good at searching fast through text or lists for a specific word or phrase. They are therefore used to write accounting packages and spreadsheets.

Other computer languages, such as Lisp and Prolog, fall into a different category. These languages give the programmer less scope for writing mathematical, accounting or scientific applications; instead they allow you to manipulate ideas, names and words as symbols. They are therefore called symbolic programming languages.

SYNTAX

NLP

Syntax deals with the formal arrangement of words in a sentence, without regard to their meaning. The words in an English sentence can only be combined in certain ways. Thus the sentence:

The pig flew over the garden fence

is syntactically correct, but the sentence:

Pig flied garden fence the over

conflicts with the rules of English grammar and so is syntactically wrong. Contrast syntax with *semantics* which is concerned with meaning. Even if the syntax of a sentence is right, it may not actually make any sense. The semantics of the sentence:

The apple tasted very yellow

is certainly dubious, even though its syntax is correct.

See also: Grammar, Parser

TASK ASSIGNMENT PROBLEM

Games and
toy domains

This is a problem which has been a test bed for planning programs. Several people perform several tasks with different speeds. What distribution of people between tasks gets the overall job done fastest? This problem suffers from the combinatorial explosion, because the number of ways of assigning N tasks to N people is N factorial. For a realistic planning exercise, with 50 tasks, the number of combinations is about 10^{64}. Searching all these is

	John	Mary	Jo
Filing	1	1·5	2
Typing	2·5	4	2
Mail	1·5	3	4

Relative efficiency

Filing   John

Typing   Mary

Mail   Jo

impractical, so this is a good model for search strategies. This is a highly connected problem, in that assigning a person to a task limits what other people can do. Thus the problem cannot easily be broken down into sub-tasks. Like the *travelling salesman problem*, the task-assignment problem has been approached with some success by neural nets, which are well suited to highly connected problems.

See also: Combinatorial explosion

TECHNICAL WORKSTATION

General
computer
term

A technical workstation is a type of computer used mainly for research and development of software.

In the late 1970s and early 1980s, there was a trend towards high-performance computers for developing particular types of application. For example, the company Symbolics bought out the Symbolics 3600, a specialized Lisp machine designed exclusively for developing programs written in Symbolics Lisp. These specialized machines were fairly expensive; more general technical workstations became popular as a cheaper alternative.

Technical workstations typically run under the Unix operating system. They have large, high-resolution screens and several megabytes of RAM. Many AI applications need large amounts of memory to run: symbolic computation requires more memory than conventional programs to run.

See also: Development tool

TEXTURE

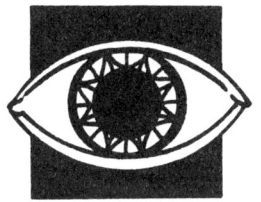

Vision

The surface texture of an object can give a computer vision system important clues about that object's identity and orientation. Most objects can be distinguished from the background on which they are resting by their texture,

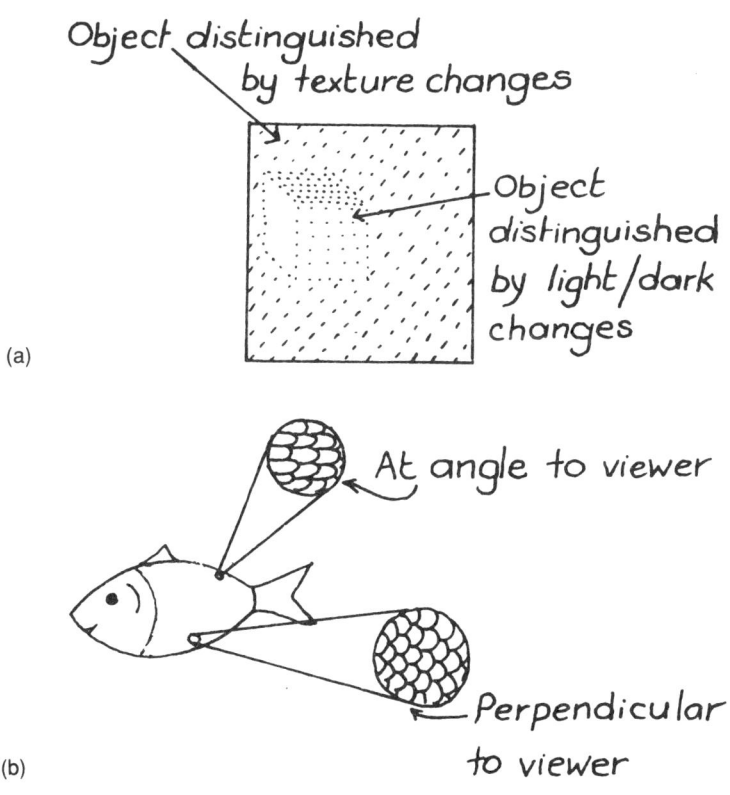

Object distinguished by texture changes

Object distinguished by light/dark changes

(a)

At angle to viewer

Perpendicular to viewer

(b)

if not their colour or lightness. However, distinguishing texture is difficult. Texture is something that only an area can be said to have. So to define bits of an image as having different textures, we are attempting to define an area in terms of a property held by that area.

Once identified, the texture of a region can give clues about its orientation in space, by comparing it to the texture of the untilted surface. This presupposes that the program knows what the untilted surface looks like. It can assume that most surfaces are isotropic (as our own vision systems do): i.e. all the sub-areas within them are the same. An apparent change in some property is therefore due to a change in orientation. Alternatively, you can assume that any ellipses you see are actually circles viewed at an angle, that any rectangles are squares at an angle and so on. Lastly, the vision system could have a database of what the 'flat' texture of a surface looks like.

See also: Depth

TOY DOMAINS AND PUZZLES

Games and
toy domains

These are both terms for test systems on which AI programs have cut their teeth.

Games and puzzles do not necessarily have a counterpart in the real world, but illustrate some logical point or procedural problem. There are a vast number of puzzles and games used in AI: some of the more widely used are discussed under *Classic puzzles*.

Toy domains are simplifications of a real-life situation, such as *blocks world* (which supposes the world to be composed solely of geometrically regular blocks). Another type is the *travelling salesman problem*.

See also: Classic puzzles, Task-assignment problem, Travelling salesman problem

TRAINING EXAMPLE

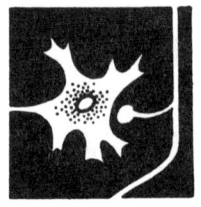

Neural nets

A training example is the 'data' you provide a neural net. Most neural-net simulations are quite flexible, with the connection weights between neurones unspecified when the program is started. In order for a neural net to recognize a pattern (the most common and most successful use of neural nets), it must be taught what the pattern looks like. This is done by showing it a series of examples of the target pattern, called training examples. While it is being shown these another input is set so that the net treats these as typical examples of a particular category of object, and after it has been shown each example it adjusts the synaptic weights of its neurones according to the match between its output and the output desired. After a number of these examples (the number depending on how many patterns you require the net to be able to recognize and how many neurones there are in it), the net has learned to recognize that pattern (to some degree of accuracy).

See also: Neural nets

TRANSFORMATIONAL GRAMMAR

NLP

Transformational grammar was conceived in 1957 by the linguist Chomsky at MIT and has undergone continuous study and elaboration ever since.

Transformational grammar works in two stages. First, it uses a very simple idea called 'context-free grammar' to generate all the possible sentences from a given number of words.

It then adds a level of sophistication by applying rules to the sentences generated. Thus, by applying a series of rules, the sentences:

The cat sits on the mat
The cat was sitting on the mat
The cats were sitting on the mats

might be generated from the original sentence:

The cat sat on the mat

The context-free structure grammar is said to generate the deep structure of the sentence. The transformations of the deep structure are surface structures: sentences which have similarity of meaning but, for example, different tenses, plural nouns and slightly different wording.

See also: Grammar, Parser

217

TRAVELLING SALESMAN PROBLEM

Games and
toy domains

This is one of the standard problems whose solution is a test of many approaches to AI problem-solving. A salesman must visit each of a number of cities on a 'tour', starting and finishing at the same city and visiting all the others only once. What is the shortest route he can take?

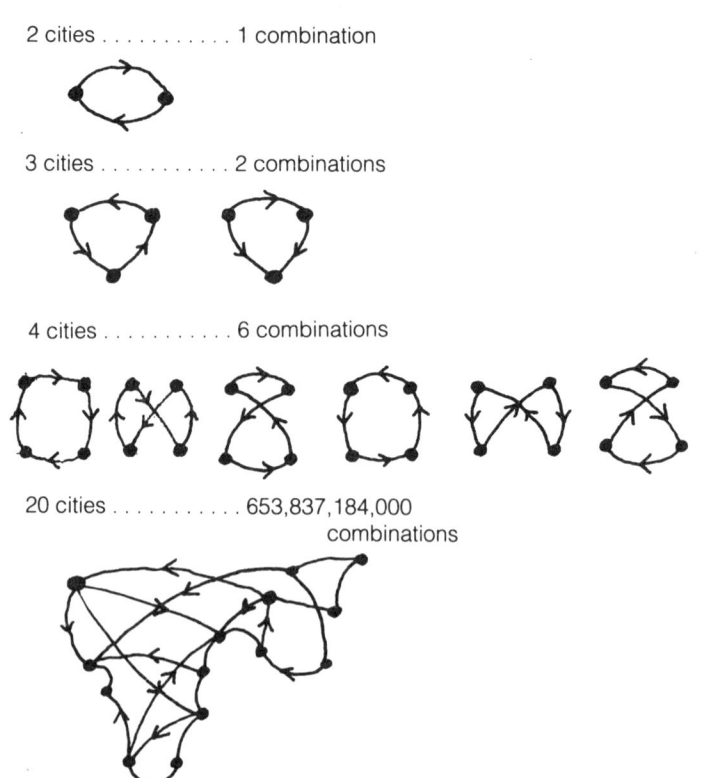

This problem is difficult because of its potential size: there is a combinatorial explosion if you work out all the number of routes possible for a large number of cities. You cannot divide it into sub-problems because which city you visit next depends on which cities you have visited so far. This interdependency means that it is also ideally suited to neural-net approaches, rather than conventional game-playing methods, as illustrated by J. J. Hopfield's TSP neural net which finds a nearly optimal solution to the TSP in a few machine cycles.

TUPLE

Prog.
techniques

In computer applications, a tuple is a single record containing some items that go together in a certain order. A pair of map coordinates might be a tuple, in this case a 2-tuple because there are two items (in the case of pairs they are usually called 'ordered pairs'). In general, an *n*-tuple is an ordered list of *n* items.

A tuple is often a parameter in a program. It is a way of passing several items of information as an argument when you are only allowed one parameter.

Some programming systems for parallel computers have programs and data organized not as a linear list of items like a conventional computer program but as a collection of lists in no particular order. The lists themselves are called tuples and the whole program can be viewed as a 'sea' of tuples from which the computer fishes whatever it needs in the way of data and program segments when it needs them.

If tuples seem suspiciously like lists to you, they do to us too.

See also: List processing

TURING MACHINE

Theory/
Philosophy

The Turing machine is an automaton. It is a simple, theoretical computer designed to test what computers can and cannot do. A Turing machine has a very small memory (called the machine's 'internal state') and a very small instruction set. Its only input and output is via a 'head' which scans along a paper tape of characters, reading a character or writing one on the tape. The machine can also move left or right along the tape when instructed to do so by its program and 'memory'.

Alan Turing, the machine's inventor in the 1930s, showed that, with a long enough tape, a Turing machine could do anything that could be done 'by definite methods' (what we would now call discrete electronics, including digital computers). Thus it had full computational power, and is a model for all digital computers.

See also: Automaton

TURING TEST

Theory/
Philosophy

This test was devised by Alan Turing as a 'thought experiment' to determine whether it was sensible to talk about an 'intelligent computer'. He envisaged two teletypes in two rooms, connected to each other. You, the tester, sat at one, and typed questions into it. You received answers. If, after some predetermined time, you could not distinguish between the answers you were getting and those that a human would produce, then whatever was typing the answers had to be presumed to be intelligent.

Turing considered that this test focused attention on the essence of intelligence, and so helped to define what an intelligent computer (or as we would now say, an intelligent program) would have to do. In fact it is a formalized version of what goes on in court-rooms and job interviews all the time, when one human tries to find out what processes are taking place inside another's head by asking questions.

The test could be fooled by programs which simulate rather than emulate human thought. It also assumes that *Homo sapiens* is the ideal yardstick of intelligence, something that even Turing (who eventually was driven to suicide by his fellow men) might consider open to discussion.

See also: Simulation v. emulation, Chinese room

2½D SKETCH

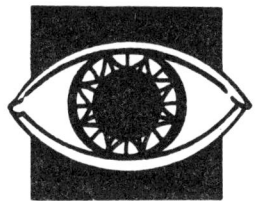

Vision

The penultimate step in a vision processing system, a 2½D sketch is a picture which contains all the three-dimensional information which can be extracted from the image, but no other. Thus a 2½D sketch of a box would show the front facing the computer, and the top and side sloping away from it, but not the back, which can only be deduced from the picture together with database knowledge about the actual, full shape of boxes. The complete picture, with all sides, is called a 3D sketch.

A related usage of the 2½D sketch occurs in CAD (computer-aided design). Here a 2½D sketch is one where a complex 3D object is displayed on a flat VDU screen by various devices (such as 'hidden lines'), but with no full representation of the object as a 3D object inside the computer. A 3D sketch, by contrast, derives from a full representation of the object inside the computer as a 3D object. This requires more information, but usually produces more realistic images.

See also: Depth

VIRTUAL MACHINE

General
computer
term

A virtual machine is the way a computer appears to behave to the user, as opposed to the way it actually works. Thus a user of a time-sharing computer may really be sharing it with 46 others, but it does not look that way, as they can all work apparently uninterrupted. Each user also apparently has a large 'virtual memory' available, although in reality they have a small bit of the real memory and a much larger slice of disk space as 'pretend memory'.

A related but distinct usage is the emulation of one computer inside another computer. The user thinks that she is using the simulated computer while in fact she is using some other machine entirely, one that operates in a logically identical way by simulating all of the other computer's set of machine-code instructions.

VISION

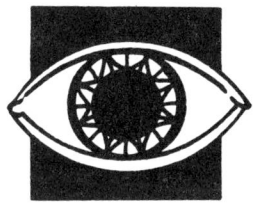

Vision

Vision is the means by which machines are (or will be) enabled to use data which they collect from a remote sensor of some sort, most usually a light detector. It is sometimes divided into

1. *machine vision*, which is the mechanical parts of it, and
2. *computer vision*, which is the data-processing parts

(although machine vision is often used for the whole process). AI is concerned almost exclusively with the second part.

Traditional AI vision systems derive substantially from the work of David Marr, who outlined a step-wise approach to analysing an image at increasing size scales. Among the problems to be solved in this approach are the following.

1. *Feature identification.* A feature is any part of an image that is in some way distinctive, such as a plane or an edge. Features can be classified into scene features (tilt, lighting intensity and direction) and image features (planes, lines). The image-processing steps of segmentation and edge detection build up a repertoire of the features present in an image, which are then combined for identification of objects.
2. *Object identification.* What does that shadow actually represent? Related to this is
3. *Object orientation.* Which way round is it? This is of considerable practical importance in robotics.
4. *Depth.* How far away is it?
5. *Hidden objects.* Just because I cannot see all four legs on a gnu, does it mean I have found a three-legged gnu?
6. *Motion.* How do I decide that this gnu over here is the same gnu as I saw a moment ago over there?

225

Other entries on vision fit into two lines of thought. Traditional vision systems start with a *binary image*, a black-and-white image from which *edge detection* extracts the edges of bits of the image, and are used to construct a *primal sketch*. This delimits areas of the image, which is *segmented* into image segments. *Depth* information, telling how far the bits of the image are away from the camera, are combined with surface *texture* elements to build up a $2^1/_2D$ *sketch*, a half-way house to a full 3D representation of the scene.

Other approaches are *model-based vision* and *neural-net* methods.

VOICE RECOGNITION

General
computer
term

This is the decoding of a speech signal for input into a computer. Voice recognition is not, actually, the recognition of voices but the recognition of what they are saying, i.e. of speech.

The problem falls into two parts: acoustic-phonetic and linguistic. The latter is the realm of *natural-language processing*. The former is how to decode a series of sounds into something equivalent to the typewritten data fed into most NLP systems. This decoding process is complicated by the way that speech slurs one syllable into another, so that each item of sound (phoneme) is not enunciated separately, isolated from its neighbours by a short silence, but is blended into them and indeed altered by them. Thus identification of the divisions between words can be quite difficult. Humans do this in part by translating the words as they go along. Incorrect segmentation can result in incorrect translation.

VON NEUMANN MACHINE

Theory/
Philosophy

A type of computer, a von Neumann machine is a 'traditional' computer. In particular, it is one that

1. has the following basic components:
   (a) a control unit;
   (b) an arithmetic and logic unit;
   (c) memory;
   (d) input and output units;
2. stores programs and data in the same memory (note that this does not necessarily mean in the same *place* in memory, just in the same type of box);
3. has control and arithmetic and logic units which determine what the computer is going to do next according to instructions read from memory in a defined sequence.

This leads to the idea of a program as a set of instructions in memory, one of which is the 'next' instruction identified by a program counter. It is also a description of a serial computer, although in practice some parallel computers, particularly array or vector processors, can be considered as a lot of serial, von Neumann computers talking to each other.

Thus nearly all actual computers are von Neumann machines. Ones that are not include dataflow computers (where the instruction to be performed next is determined not by a program counter but by the availability of data for the instructions) and neural nets (where control, arithmetic and memory functions are all served by one type of unit, the 'neurone').

See also: Serial, Parallel processing

ZERO SUM

Games and
toy domains

Zero sum, or zerosum, is the name given to a type of game, also called a 'constant-sum' game. It is a term deriving from games theory. A zero-sum game is one in which the total amount available to win is constant, so if one player wins more, the other inevitably loses more. An election is a zero-sum game: if one candidate wins, the other *must* lose. The idea of a zero-sum game is important in analysing some sorts of problem, like population genetics, crowd control and elections, but it is mainly used for various games.

A related term is *symmetric game* (and its converse, *asymmetric game*). In a symmetric game the players are exactly equal, so that, if they both have the same choices, it does not matter which player makes which choice. Chess is an example of such a game: the same moves are available to each player, so it does not matter which one you call black and which white. Poker is an asymmetric game, as one player has the advantage of being the dealer. (In fact, chess is not absolutely symmetric, as one player has to start.)

Appendix A: Benchmark AI Programs

A few AI programs have become standards in their area of AI. They are often quoted as examples of approaches to problem-solving, and so are listed here together with their start dates, main authors (or, where the programs have been the result of an extended project, the affiliation of the various workers), and the field of AI they are meant to typify.

Program	Date	Author(s)	Subject area
ACRONYM	1981	Brooks	Model-based, domain-independent interpretation system. Half-way between a program and a language, it identifies and classifies objects to compare with a database of graph descriptions. Used in vision research.
CHI	1981	Kestrel Institute	Automatic programming tool using a variety of methods to provide a 'friendly', interactive, natural-language programming environment. Successor to PSI.
CONGEN	1976	Stanford Univesity	Updated version of DENDRAL which could deal with cyclic chemical structures.

Program	Date	Author(s)	Subject area
DEDELUS	1975	Richard Waldinger and Zohar Manna	Automatic programming system which takes a very high-level, logical, complete program specification and produces a program in Lisp to satisfy it.
DENDRAL	1965	Stanford University	Heuristic expert system to deduce the structures of non-cyclic chemical compounds from their mass spectra (MS). A relatively simple algorithm can generate all possible structures: the program uses MS results to constrain the structures it actually tries.
ELIZA	1966	Joseph Weizenbaum	Early NLP program, which mimicked a non-directive psychoanalyst by picking out key words in the typed input and printing out modifications of a stock of standard phrases.
EMYCIN	1980	Stanford University	Expert system shell, with the control structures of MYCIN but with MYCIN's infectious-disease database removed.
GPS	1957	Newell, Shaw and Simon	The general problem solver, using means-end analysis to solve suitably formulated problems. Ran into difficulties with the generalization of its internal representation of its subject-matter.

Program	Date	Author(s)	Subject area
GUIDON	1978	William Clancey	CAI program for infectious disease, using MYCIN's database as the subject and a separate database of 200 tutoring rules to guide teaching activities. Also has an internal model of the student's partial knowledge.
HACKER	1975	Gerald Sussman	A learning system that learns to produce a plan (to guide a robot to stack blocks) by doing simulated dry runs to compile a list of known 'dos' and 'don'ts'. This is a model of learning programming skills.
HARPY	1975	Carnegie Mellon University	Speech-understanding program that contains a pre-compiled semantic, syntactic and phonetic knowledge about all the sentences it recognizes.
HEARSAY	1976	ARPA-funded program	Speech-understanding program based on a blackboard structure with independent modules for acoustic/phonetic syntactic and semantic knowledge.
INTERNIST	1974	H. Pople and J. Myers	Consultation expert system in internal medicine. It takes patient observations and deduces a list of compatible disease states based on a tree database linking diseases and symptoms.

Program	Date	Author(s)	Subject area
LEX	1981	Thomas Mitchell	Learns to solve simple maths integration problems by discovering heuristic rules about when to apply an in-built database of basic integration functions.
LUNAR	1972	Bolt, Beranek and Newman Inc.	An NLP system that uses an ATN parser to translate English queries into a formal query language to extract information from a database of facts on the Apollo 11 moon rock samples. It is therefore a NLP 'front end'.
MACIE	1986		Matrix-controlled inference engine. Stand-alone expert system inference engine for use with connectionist models of knowledge bases.
MACSYMA	1971	MIT and users	Large interactive symbolic manipulation program for problem-solving in mathematics. The program can perform over 600 mathematical operations including equation solution, Taylor-series expansion, matrix and vector algebra. It has its own programming language, and a vast knowledge base.
META-DENDRAL	1978	Stanford University	Program to derive rules for use by DENDRAL. It infers from being given the mass spectrometry data generated by known molecules, by

Program	Date	Author(s)	Subject area
			induction, starting with very general rules and making them increasingly specific.
MYCIN	1976	Stanford University	Consultative expert system on infectious disease diagnosis. Probably the most famous expert system, it uses production rules, with certainty values attached to diagnoses, to capture knowledge. Deduction is by backward chaining resulting in an exhaustive depth-first search of its rules base for relevant rules.
PROSPECTOR	1978	SRI International	Consultation expert system to assist geologists. Knowledge is stored as a network with nodes = assertions and arcs = inference rules. Gained fame in 1982 by proving more accurate than human geologists in interpreting a field survey.
PSI	1979	Cordell Green and others	Automatic programming system incorporating a wide range of methods into a 'supportive programming environment'. Program is specified by mixed-initiative dialogue which provides the specification for use by a set of closely interacting 'experts' in different knowledge areas.

Program	Date	Author(s)	Subject area
QMR	1980	Popple	Microcomputer version of INTERNIST. Uses frame-based database.
SCHOLAR	1970	Bolt, Beranek and Newman Inc.	Tutoring system for teaching South American geography. Used mixed-initiative English sentences to test students on knowledge held in the program as semantic nets. By not making the closed-world assumption, SCHOLAR allows for the incompleteness of its database.
SHRDLU	1972	Terry Winograd	Natural-language system which could hold discussions about an internally represented 'blocks world'. The parser element worked on systemic grammar. SHRDLU bypassed some of the more complex features of English by restricting its domain and incorporating powerful problem-solving techniques; it is doubtful if it could be extended to wider domains.
SOPHIE	1975	Bolt, Beranek and Newman Inc.	CAI program in electronics. Acts as combination of tutor and simulated workbench. Natural-language interface uses a semantic grammar to tell the student what her circuit is doing, and test and

Program	Date	Author(s)	Subject area
			criticize the student's hypotheses about the reasons for the results she gets.
STRIPS	1971	Richard Fikes and Nils Nilsson	Problem-solving program which uses predicate calculus to solve problems concerning the movement of a robot about a series of rooms. The actual and desired organization of the room contents are represented by nodes on a state graph, which STRIPS searches for paths between current state and goal.
SYSTRAN	1978		Machine-translation package. Sentences are partially translated into an internal representation which is then translated back to a surface structure in another language.
TEIRESIAS	1975	Randall Davis	A system that assists entry of data into large databases. TEIRESIAS is a learning program that incorporates knowledge from an expert into a knowledge base (originally MYCIN). Internal meta-rules direct the acqusition of database items.
WUSOR	1979	Ira Goldstein and Brian Carr	Coach to teach the playing of the computer game WUMPUS. The program has an internal model of the student, which relies on a game expert module to

Program	Date	Author(s)	Subject area
			provide information about the game and psychology and tutor modules to guide teaching.
XCON	1978	Digital Equipment Corporation	Expert system to configure VAX 11/780 computers. Also called R1. Various techniques used in construction (leading to a complete rewrite in 1986–7).

Appendix B: AI Languages and Environments

A few languages or programming environments appear a number of times in discussions of AI. Here we list a few of the more common, and their attributes.

Language/environment	Description
ART	Programming environment for developing expert systems, including ready-made modules in the 'shell'. Knowledge is represented in frames, rules and procedures, in many computer languages, integrated through an object-orientated 'dictionary'. Graphics interface shows logical reasoning in real time.
Conniver	Database system that stores information as a context tree: the tree simultaneously shows the different effects of possible actions. Also has pattern-matching abilities.
Expert	Expert-system-building tool to create rules-based systems. Has special facilities to enter and analyse test cases, and suggest new rules based on them. Features rapid prototyping and high-level rules entry language. Written in Fortran.
InterLisp	Commonly used version of Lisp developed by BBN and Xerox, with additional facilities such as methods for keeping track of the user's commands, procedures and file packages.

Language/environment	Description
IPL	First list-processing language, developed in 1957; introduced the idea of a list of cells and a generator which would generate all elements of some series. The GPS project was written in IPL.
KEE	'Knowledge engineering environment'. A sophisticated knowledge, database, modelling and inference tool. It combines frame-based knowledge representation, rules-based reasoning, Lisp and interactive graphics, with object-oriented programming models being used throughout.
Linda	Research programming language for the Connection Machine, using a tuple-space representation in which the elements of the program can interact freely and separately with each other in parallel.
Lisp	Language based on list structures. See glossary entry.
Loops	A general tool for constructing knowledge-based programs, Loops combines procedure-orientated, object-orientated and access-orientated programming ideas in a rules-based programming environment.
Occam	Language developed to exploit the parallel computing power of the Inmos transputer chip.
OPS5	General-purpose production-rule language. A single working memory keeps data ordered according to time of entry or modification, using this time to help resolve conflicts. The rules interpreter is very fast, but interfaces tend to be difficult to write. R1 was written in OPS5.
Planner	Language for procedural representation of knowledge in databases. The programmer expresses knowledge as a set of statements ('theorems') about procedures to adopt in specific circumstances. Has automatic backtracking ability. Implemented as

Language/environment	Description
	Micro-Planner for Terry Winograd's SHRDLU.
POP-2	Popular AI language in Britain, scarcely used elsewhere. Has many features of Lisp, together with dynamic lists, which act as generators (see IPL), and some control-structure extensions.
Prolog	Language based on predicate logic. See glossary entry.
Sail	'Stanford Artificial Intelligence Language'. Language based on Algol 60 (a now defunct contemporary of early Fortran), this has evolved into a language that has a 'traditional' control structure but with abilities to use lists, macros, co-routining, powerful associative data-retrieval facilities and an interactive debugging facility.

Index

Index